Time Inside the Mind: Age, Memory, and Human Psychological Evolution

Time Inside the Mind:

Age, Memory, and Human Psychological Evolution

Time Inside the Mind: Age, Memory, and Human Psychological Evolution

Published By: Wissira Research Lab LLC

Imprint Name: Wissira Press

US Office: Carmel, United States- 46074

India Office: KDP, RNE, India-201017

Email: editor@wissira.us, **Website:** https://books.wissira.us

Mobile: +91 7535 916 555

Prof. Dr. Anu Kant Mital

ISBN - 978-93-7559-316-4

Maharaja Agrasen Himalayan Garhwal University,

Address: Uttarakhand, India

Edition: 2026

Printed In: India

Maharaja Agrasen Himalayan Garhwal University,

Address: Uttarakhand, India

Time Inside the Mind:

Age, Memory, and Human Psychological Evolution

2026

Author:

Prof. Dr. Anu Kant Mital

Published By

Wissira Research Lab

ISBN 978-93-7559-316-4

9 789375 593164

Preface

Time is one of the most familiar yet mysterious elements of human existence. We measure it precisely with clocks and calendars, yet we experience it subjectively-sometimes flowing effortlessly, sometimes stretching unbearably, and at other moments slipping away before we realize it has passed. This book, ***Time Inside the Mind: Age, Memory, and Human Psychological Evolution*** , is born from the recognition that time is not merely an external dimension, but a deeply psychological phenomenon shaped by memory, emotion, development, culture, and biology.

The central aim of this book is to explore how human beings *experience* time across the lifespan. From the earliest moments of childhood, when the present dominates awareness, to later life, where reflection and reminiscence give time its depth and meaning, our relationship with time continually evolves. Memory acts as the thread that binds these stages together, allowing the past to inform the present and the future to be imagined. Understanding this dynamic relationship between time and memory offers valuable insight into human identity, decision-making, emotional regulation, and psychological well-being.

This book takes an interdisciplinary approach, drawing upon cognitive psychology, developmental science, neuroscience, sociology, and evolutionary perspectives. Rather than treating time as a fixed entity, the chapters examine how subjective time is shaped by cognitive growth, emotional intensity, routine, aging, cultural norms, and technological change. Special attention is given to how modern life-characterized by speed, digital memory, and extended longevity-is reshaping our temporal consciousness in unprecedented ways.

The content is structured to move progressively through the human lifespan, while also situating individual experience within broader biological and cultural frameworks. Each chapter is designed to be conceptually clear and empirically grounded, making the book suitable for undergraduate and postgraduate students, researchers, educators, and readers with a general interest in psychology and human behaviour. Real-world examples and contemporary research are used to bridge theory and lived experience.

This book is an invitation to examine the machinery behind that travel. It explores the tension between *Kronos* (quantitative, linear time) and *Kairos* (the qualitative, opportune moment). By bridging these concepts, we reveal why a childhood summer felt like an eternity, while a year in middle age vanishes in a blink.

The methodology behind this volume is rooted in the "Tripartite Model of Temporal Experience": the biological clock, the cognitive processor, and the social construct. We delve into the neurochemical messengers, like dopamine, that speed up our internal metronome during moments of excitement, and the inhibitory processes that slow it down during boredom or trauma. Furthermore, we address the "scarcity mindset"—the psychological state of feeling that time is a vanishing resource—and how this impacts our decision-making, from financial investments to romantic commitments.

Ultimately, *Time Inside the Mind* invites readers to reflect on their own relationship with time. By understanding how the mind constructs and interprets temporal experience, we gain the ability not only to study human psychological evolution but also to live more consciously within the time we have. This book hopes to encourage thoughtful engagement with the rhythms of memory, aging, and change that define the human journey.

Author:

Prof. Dr. Anu Kant Mital

Overview of the Book

Time Inside the Mind: Age, Memory, and Human Psychological Evolution offer a comprehensive exploration of how human beings perceive, experience, and interpret time across the lifespan. Rather than treating time as a purely physical or chronological construct, the book positions time as a psychological phenomenon-shaped by memory, emotion, cognition, culture, and biological development. At its core, the book argues that understanding the human mind requires understanding how time is internally constructed and lived.

The book begins by establishing the psychological foundations of time perception. Early chapters examine how subjective time differs from objective clock time and how cognitive processes such as attention, emotion, and memory influence the experience of duration and sequence. Memory is presented as the central mechanism that gives time meaning, enabling continuity of identity and the capacity to mentally revisit the past or imagine the future.

Layer 1: The Internal Engine (Chapters 1–2)

In these initial chapters, we break down the "Scalar Expectancy Theory," which explains how our brain's internal pacemaker pulses and how those pulses are "counted" by our attention. We investigate the "Holiday Paradox"—the strange phenomenon where a novel trip feels long in retrospect because of the density of new memories, even if it felt fast while occurring. This section provides the technical vocabulary needed to understand the "Architecture of the Mind," specifically focusing on the hippocampus as the brain's primary chronometer.

Layer 2: The Lifespan Trajectory (Chapters 3–6)

This segment serves as the heart of the book, detailing the "temporal milestones" of human growth. In Chapter 3, we analyze "infantile amnesia" and why the lack of a narrative self in early childhood prevents the formation of long-term temporal anchors. Moving into adolescence (Chapter 4), we discuss the "Reminiscence Bump"—the psychological tendency for adults to have the most vivid and frequent memories from their teenage and early adult years.

Chapter 5 explores "Time Compression" in adulthood, arguing that as life becomes more predictable and "chunked" into routines, the brain stops encoding new "time markers," causing years to feel shorter. Chapter 6 provides a counter-narrative to aging, focusing on "Socioemotional Selectivity Theory." This explains how, as the horizon of life narrows, older adults prioritize emotionally meaningful goals over knowledge-acquisition goals, leading to a profound shift in temporal value.

Layer 3: The Global and Future Horizon (Chapters 7–9)

The final third of the book elevates the discussion from the individual to the species. Chapter 7 provides a rigorous look at the **Neuroscience of Time**, detailing how the suprachiasmatic nucleus regulates our circadian rhythms and what happens when this "master clock" desynchronizes. Chapter 8 shifts to a macroscopic view, comparing "Monochronic" cultures (linear, promptness-oriented) with "Polychronic" cultures (fluid, relationship-oriented), and how these cultural lenses dictate our social stress levels.

Beyond individual development, the book situates psychological time within broader neural, cultural, and evolutionary contexts. It explores how brain systems support time perception and memory across life stages, how societies and cultures shape temporal orientation, and how evolutionary pressures gave rise to human foresight and reflective consciousness. These perspectives highlight that time perception is not only personal but also socially and biologically embedded.

The final chapters turn toward the future, examining how technology, artificial intelligence, digital memory, and increased longevity are reshaping human temporal consciousness. By addressing ethical and psychological implications of memory enhancement and extended lifespans, the book raises critical questions about how human psychological evolution may unfold in a rapidly changing world.

Table of Contents

1

Time as a Psychological Construct

1.1 Objective Time vs. Subjective Time

Time exists both as a measurable external reality and as an internal psychological experience. Objective time is governed by clocks and calendars, remaining constant regardless of human perception. Subjective time, however, is shaped by attention, emotion, and cognition.

Time can be understood through two fundamentally different lenses: as an external, measurable phenomenon and as an internal, psychological experience. **Objective time** refers to the standardized measurement of duration using clocks, calendars, and physical units such as seconds and hours. It operates independently of human awareness and progresses at a constant rate, forming the basis for scientific observation, social coordination, and daily routines. Whether a person is awake, asleep, engaged, or distracted, objective time continues uninterrupted and uniform.

In contrast, **subjective time** reflects how individuals *experience* the passage of time. This psychological sense of time is deeply influenced by mental states such as attention, emotion, motivation, and cognitive workload. When a person is deeply absorbed in an engaging activity, time may appear to pass rapidly, whereas monotonous or stressful situations can make even short intervals feel extended. Emotional intensity plays a particularly important role-fear, anxiety, or anticipation can stretch perceived time, while pleasure and flow states often compress it.

Subjective time is not linear; instead, it is flexible and context-dependent. The mind continuously adjusts temporal perception based on expectations, prior experiences, and current goals. This elasticity explains why the same duration can be perceived differently by different individuals or even by the same person under varying circumstances. Importantly, subjective time is closely tied to memory formation and future planning. Events that feel longer or more intense are often remembered more vividly, while rapidly perceived periods may leave fewer memory traces. Thus, the interaction between objective and subjective time reveals that while time may be fixed in the physical world, its psychological experience is dynamic, personal, and shaped by the inner workings of the human mind.

Example: Objective Time vs. Subjective Time

Consider two students sitting for the same **60-minute examination**. From an objective perspective, the duration of the exam is identical for both-exactly one hour measured by the clock. However, their **subjective experience of time** differs significantly.

- **Student A** is well prepared and confident. As they focus on answering questions, their attention is fully engaged. For this student, the exam feels as though it ends quickly, and they are surprised when the invigilator announces that time is up. Subjectively, the hour feels short and compressed.
- **Student B**, on the other hand, feels anxious and unprepared. They frequently check the clock, struggle to recall information, and experience stress throughout the exam. Each minute feels slow and heavy, making the same one-hour period feel much longer than it actually is.

In both cases, **objective time remains constant**, but **subjective time varies** based on emotional state, attention, and cognitive engagement. This example illustrates how psychological factors shape the personal experience of time, even when external time measurement does not change.

1.2 Mental Timekeeping and Cognitive Processing

The human mind relies on internal mechanisms to track duration, sequence, and temporal order. These processes allow individuals to estimate intervals, plan actions, and coordinate behaviour.

Mental timekeeping refers to the brain's ability to perceive, estimate, and organize time without relying on external devices such as clocks or calendars. This internal timing capacity allows individuals to judge how long an activity lasts, recognize the order of events, and anticipate what should happen next. Such temporal awareness is essential for everyday functioning, from managing conversations and routines to executing complex tasks that require sequencing and coordination.

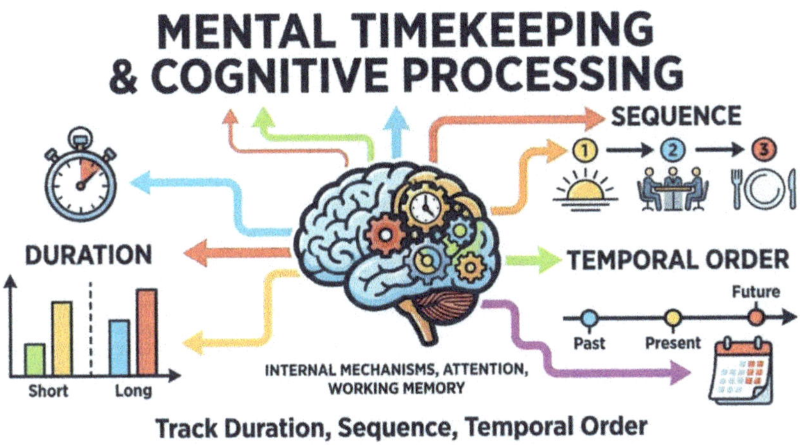

Cognitive processes play a central role in this internal sense of time. **Attention** acts as a key regulator: when individuals focus closely on a task, the brain can more accurately register the passage of time. Conversely, when attention is divided-such as during multitasking or distraction-time judgments tend to become distorted, often leading to overestimation or underestimation of duration. **Working memory** also supports mental timekeeping by holding temporal information temporarily, enabling people to compare intervals, track progress, and align actions with goals.

Mental timekeeping is not merely about counting duration; it also supports **temporal structure** in thought. The mind organizes experiences into sequences, helping individuals understand cause-and-effect relationships and maintain continuity across events. This sequencing ability allows people to reflect on past experiences, remain oriented in the present, and plan for the future. Through this process, experiences are woven into coherent mental narratives rather than existing as isolated moments.

Ultimately, internal timekeeping enables humans to impose order on experience. By integrating attention, memory, and perception, the cognitive system transforms the constant flow of events into meaningful patterns. This ability to mentally track time is fundamental to learning, decision-making, and the sense of a continuous personal identity extending across past, present, and future.

Case Study: Mental Timekeeping Under Divided Attention

A frequently cited experimental case in cognitive psychology involves **dual-task performance and time estimation** , demonstrating how mental timekeeping depends on cognitive resources such as attention and working memory.

In a controlled laboratory setting, participants were asked to perform **two tasks simultaneously**. The primary task involved listening to a sequence of tones and estimating when **one minute** had passed without using any external clock. The secondary task required participants to solve simple arithmetic problems presented intermittently during the same interval. A comparison group performed only the time-estimation task without any additional cognitive load.

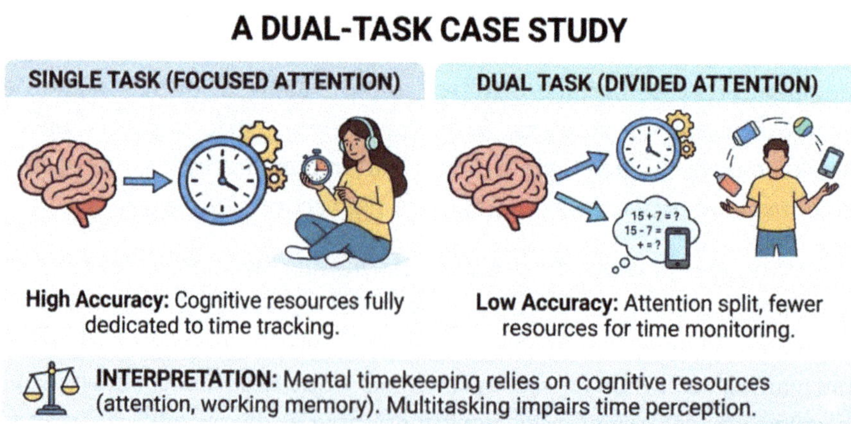

Findings:

Participants who focused solely on estimating time were able to stop the timer with relatively high accuracy, often within a few seconds of the actual one-minute mark. In contrast, participants performing both tasks consistently **misjudged the duration** , typically allowing more than one minute to pass before signalling completion. Their attention was split between problem-solving and monitoring time, reducing the cognitive resources available for internal time tracking.

Interpretation:

This case study illustrates that mental timekeeping is not an automatic or independent process. Instead, it relies heavily on attentional monitoring and working memory. When attention is diverted, fewer cognitive "markers" are registered, leading the brain to perceive that less time has passed than in reality. As a result, time estimation becomes inaccurate.

Real-World Relevance:

This phenomenon explains why people often lose track of time while multitasking-such as working on a laptop during meetings or using a smartphone while waiting. It also has implications for high-stakes environments like aviation, healthcare, and driving, where divided attention can impair not only performance but also accurate judgment of timing and sequence.

Overall, this case study reinforces the idea that mental timekeeping is deeply intertwined with cognitive processing and that accurate temporal perception depends on focused attention and available cognitive capacity.

1.3 Emotional Influence on Time Perception

Emotions significantly distort the perception of time. High-arousal emotions like fear or excitement can slow down or speed up subjective time. For example, threatening situations often feel prolonged due to heightened awareness, while engaging activities may compress perceived duration.

Emotions play a powerful role in shaping how time is subjectively experienced. Rather than perceiving time as a steady and uniform flow, the human mind adjusts temporal perception based on emotional intensity and arousal. **High-arousal emotions**, such as fear, anxiety, anger, or excitement, often disrupt normal time perception, causing moments to feel either stretched or compressed depending on the situation. This explains why time rarely feels neutral during emotionally charged experiences.

In threatening or stressful situations, time often appears to **slow down**. This effect is linked to heightened alertness and increased sensory awareness. When an individual feels fear, the brain prioritizes survival, rapidly processing environmental cues and bodily signals. As more information is registered within a short objective interval, the mind interprets the experience as lasting longer. This temporal expansion can be adaptive, allowing individuals to react quickly, make split-second decisions, and avoid danger.

Conversely, **positive or engaging emotional states** -such as joy, curiosity, or deep interest-tend to make time feel as though it passes quickly. During enjoyable activities, attention is absorbed by the experience itself rather than by monitoring time. As a result, fewer conscious temporal markers are formed, leading to a sense of time compression. This is commonly experienced during creative work, social interactions, or leisure activities that induce a state of flow.

Emotion also shapes how time is perceived **in memory**. Events associated with strong emotions are often remembered as lasting longer than neutral ones, even if their actual duration was brief. Emotional salience enhances memory encoding, making such moments more vivid and detailed in retrospect. Through this mechanism, emotional experiences leave stronger cognitive imprints, reinforcing learning and guiding future behaviour.

Overall, the interaction between emotion and time perception highlights the adaptive function of psychological time. By flexibly adjusting temporal experience based on emotional relevance, the mind enhances survival, decision-making, and learning-demonstrating that time perception is not merely a passive process but an active, emotion-sensitive cognitive function.

1.4 Time Perception as an Adaptive Function

From an evolutionary perspective, flexible time perception has survival value. The ability to rapidly assess danger or endure waiting periods supports adaptive decision-making. Psychological time allows humans to anticipate consequences, delay gratification, and learn from past experiences.

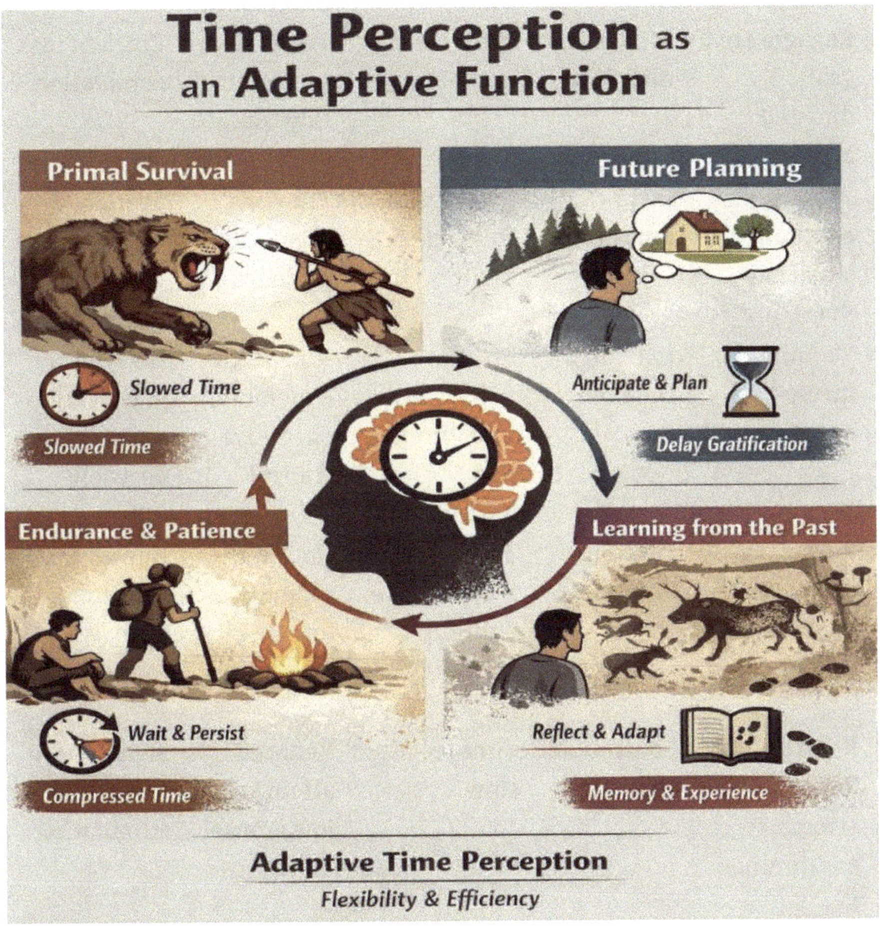

Adaptive Context	Objective Time Condition	Subjective Time Experience	Cognitive Function Involved	Evolutionary Benefit
Threat or danger (e.g., predator, accident)	Short duration	Time f eels slowed or expanded	Heightene d attention, rapid informatio n processing	Faster reactions and improved survival
Engaging or goal-directed activity	Moderate duration	Time feels compressed	Focused attention, flow state	Efficient task completion
Waiting or endurance situations	Long duration	Time feels tolerable or neutral	Emotion regulation, patience	Sustained effort without distress
Planning for future outcomes	Extended timeline	Time perceived as structured and anticipatory	Prospectiv e memory, executive control	Delayed gratification and strategic decision-making
Reflecting on past experiences	Past duration	Time reconstructe d through memory	Episodic memory, learning	Improved learning from consequence s
Routine or low-stimulus environmen t	Continuou s duration	Time feels slow	Reduced attention, low arousal	Signals need for change or stimulation

Time perception serves not merely as a passive awareness of duration but as an **adaptive psychological function** shaped by evolutionary pressures. For early humans, survival depended on the ability to respond quickly to threats, assess opportunities, and regulate behaviour across changing environmental conditions. A flexible sense of time allowed individuals to adjust their reactions according to situational demands rather than relying on a rigid perception of duration.

In dangerous or high-risk situations, the mind's tendency to **expand perceived time** enhances survival. When time feels slowed, individuals can process more information, evaluate options, and execute rapid responses such as fleeing or defending themselves. This heightened temporal sensitivity increases the likelihood of avoiding harm. Conversely, in safe or repetitive conditions, time compression enables endurance-allowing individuals to tolerate long periods of waiting, traveling, or routine labour without excessive cognitive strain.

Psychological time also plays a crucial role in **anticipation and planning**. Humans are uniquely capable of projecting themselves into the future, imagining outcomes, and adjusting present behaviour accordingly. This ability supports delayed gratification, where individuals forgo immediate rewards in Favor of long-term benefits-an essential skill for cooperation, resource management, and social organization. Similarly, reflecting on past experiences helps refine future decisions, reinforcing learning through remembered consequences.

Importantly, variability in time perception is not a cognitive weakness but a sign of **mental efficiency**. By stretching or compressing subjective time, the brain prioritizes information that is most relevant for action, learning, and survival. This adaptability allows humans to function effectively in complex, unpredictable environments. Thus, time perception emerges as a dynamic cognitive tool-one that aligns perception with purpose and enables intelligent interaction with the world.

Multiple Choice Questions (MCQs)

1. Which of the following best defines objective time?

a) Time shaped by emotions and attention
b) Time measured by clocks and calendars
c) Time remembered through past experiences
d) Time altered by cognitive bias
Answer: b) Time measured by clocks and calendars

2. Subjective time primarily depends on which factors?

a) Gravity and motion
b) Biological aging only
c) Attention, emotion, and cognition
d) Social norms
Answer: c) Attention, emotion, and cognition

3. Why does time appear to slow down during fearful situations?

a) The clock speed changes
b) Memory stops forming
c) Heightened awareness increases information processing
d) Cognitive processing shuts down
Answer: c) Heightened awareness increases information processing

4. Which cognitive resource plays a key role in mental timekeeping?

a) Long-term memory
b) Intelligence quotient
c) Working memory and attention
d) Language ability
Answer: c) Working memory and attention

5. What typically happens to time perception during engaging or enjoyable activities?

a) Time feels prolonged
b) Time feels compressed
c) Time becomes inaccurate objectively
d) Time perception disappears
Answer: b) Time feels compressed

Short Answer Questions

1. What is the difference between objective time and subjective time?
2. How does attention influence an individual's perception of time?
3. Why do emotionally intense situations often feel longer than they actually are?
4. What role does working memory play in mental timekeeping?
5. How does divided attention affect time estimation?
6. Why is psychological time considered flexible rather than linear?

Long Answer Questions

1. Discuss time as a psychological construct, explaining how objective and subjective time differ in human experience.
2. Explain the role of cognitive processes such as attention and working memory in mental timekeeping, with suitable examples.
3. Analyse how emotions influence time perception and memory formation, highlighting their adaptive significance.
4. Examine time perception as an adaptive function from an evolutionary perspective.
5. Describe how psychological time contributes to learning, planning, and delayed gratification.
6. Evaluate why variability in time perception should be viewed as a cognitive strength rather than a limitation.

2

Memory and the Architecture of the Mind

2.1 Memory as the Foundation of Temporal Experience

Memory enables humans to experience time beyond the present moment. Without memory, the past would vanish instantly, and the future would hold no meaning. Memory systems preserve experiences, allowing individuals to recall, reflect, and anticipate.

Human experience of time is deeply anchored in memory. Without the ability to remember, consciousness would be confined strictly to the present instant, with no awareness of what has already occurred or what might come next. Memory allows experiences to be stored, revisited, and mentally reconstructed, giving meaning to both the past and the future. Through remembering earlier events, individuals can compare "then" with "now," recognize change, and learn from prior outcomes.

Memory also enables anticipation. By drawing on stored experiences, people imagine future possibilities, set goals, and prepare for upcoming situations. For example, recalling past successes or failures shapes expectations and influences future decisions. In this way, memory does not merely record time but actively organizes it into a meaningful sequence.

A continuous sense of personal identity is another outcome of memory. Individuals perceive themselves as the same person over time because memories link earlier experiences with present awareness. Even though thoughts, emotions, and circumstances change, memory maintains coherence by connecting different life stages into a unified narrative.

Therefore, memory functions as a psychological bridge between past, present, and future. It transforms isolated moments into a flowing experience of time, allowing humans to reflect on what has been, understand what is, and imagine what lies ahead. Without memory, temporal experience would fragment, and the sense of a continuous self would disappear.

2.2 Types of Memory and Their Temporal Roles

Different memory systems serve distinct temporal functions. Sensory memory captures fleeting impressions, short-term memory maintains immediate information, and long-term memory preserves experiences across years.

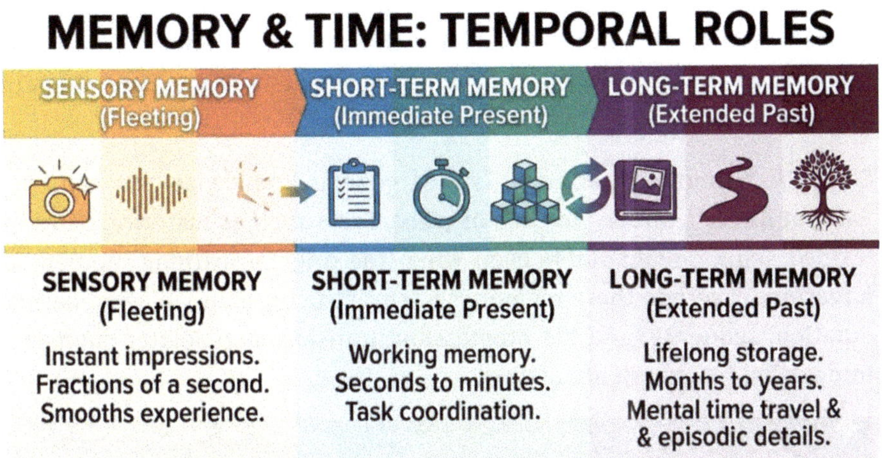

Human understanding of time is shaped by multiple memory systems, each contributing in a unique way to how experiences are processed and organized across moments, days, and years. These memory types work together to create a layered perception of temporal flow rather than a single, uniform experience.

Sensory memory operates at the shortest time scale. It briefly holds raw sensory impressions-such as sights, sounds, or textures-for fractions of a second. Although fleeting, this form of memory ensures continuity by allowing the brain to integrate rapidly changing stimuli into a smooth, ongoing present rather than disconnected fragments.

Short-term memory, often referred to as working memory, supports the immediate present. It temporarily maintains information needed for ongoing tasks, such as remembering a phone number long enough to dial it or following steps in a conversation. This system enables individuals to estimate short durations, track sequences, and coordinate actions in real time.

Long-term memory extends temporal experience across months, years, and even a lifetime. It preserves accumulated experiences and knowledge, allowing the past to remain accessible long after events have occurred. Within long-term memory, episodic memory plays a crucial temporal role by storing personal experiences along with their contextual details-when they happened, where they occurred, and how they felt. This enables mental "time travel," allowing individuals to revisit past events and compare different phases of life.

Semantic memory, in contrast, stores general knowledge and concepts without direct reference to time or place. Facts such as historical dates or learned skills remain stable even when the original learning moment is forgotten. Together, these memory systems structure human awareness of duration, sequence, and life progression, transforming isolated moments into a coherent experience of time.

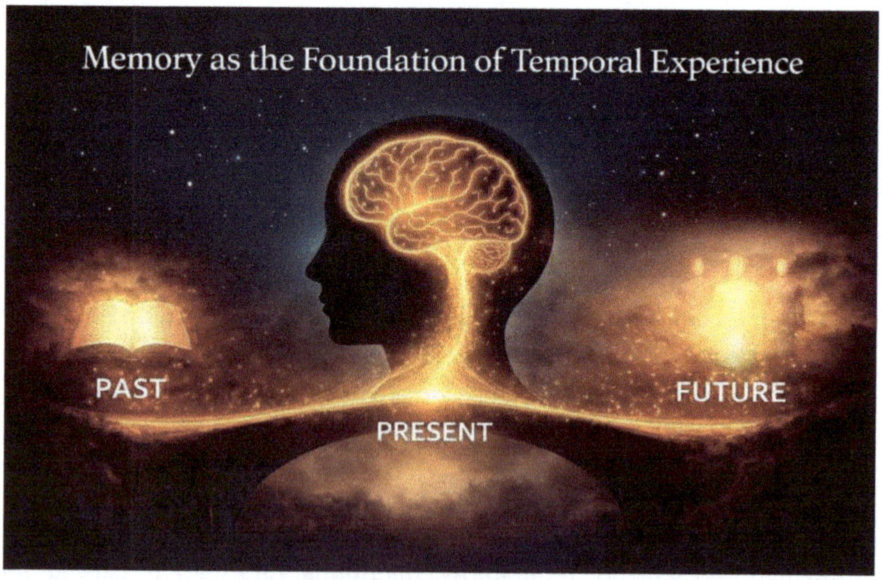

Case Study: Memory Systems and the Experience of Time in Amnesic Patients

A well-documented clinical case illustrating the temporal roles of different memory systems involves individuals with severe amnesia caused by damage to the hippocampus. One such patient was able to hold conversations, recognize objects in front of him, and respond appropriately to immediate stimuli, yet he was unable to form new long-term memories.

Observation and Findings

The patient's sensory memory and short-term memory remained largely intact. He could hear a question, understand it, and respond coherently within the moment. This showed that sensory and short-term memory systems were sufficient for maintaining a continuous present. However, once attention shifted or time passed, the experience vanished. He could not recall events that occurred just minutes earlier.

More strikingly, his episodic memory was profoundly impaired. He could not remember personal events from recent days or imagine future scenarios involving himself. When asked about plans for tomorrow, he struggled, often responding vaguely or expressing confusion. This demonstrated that episodic memory is essential not only for recalling the past but also for projecting oneself into the future.

In contrast, his semantic memory remained relatively preserved. He knew general facts, language, and social norms. He could explain what a wedding is but could not remember attending one. This separation showed that semantic memory supports timeless knowledge, while episodic memory anchors experiences within a personal timeline.

Implications

This case clearly illustrates how different memory systems contribute to temporal experience. Sensory and short-term memory sustain the immediate present, semantic memory provides stable, time-independent knowledge, and episodic memory enables continuity across past, present, and future. When episodic memory is disrupted, time collapses into an endless "now," highlighting its critical role in structuring human experience of duration, sequence, and life progression.

2.3 Memory Encoding and the Passage of Time

How experiences are encoded affects how time is later perceived. Novel or complex events generate richer memory traces, making periods appear longer in hindsight. In contrast, repetitive routines produce fewer distinctive memories, leading to the sensation that time has passed quickly.

The way experiences are encoded into memory plays a crucial role in how the passage of time is later perceived. Memory encoding refers to the process by which information from lived experiences is transformed into mental representations that can be stored and recalled. This process is not uniform; it varies depending on factors such as novelty, emotional intensity, attention, and complexity.

When individuals encounter new or stimulating situations, the brain encodes a large number of distinct details. These rich memory traces create multiple reference points in recollection. As a result, when people look back on such periods, they perceive them as longer and more expansive because many memorable events are packed into that span of time. Travel experiences, major life transitions, or first-time achievements often feel extended in hindsight for this reason.

In contrast, routine and repetitive activities demand less cognitive effort and attention. Because these experiences are encoded with fewer unique details, they leave behind sparse memory traces. When recalled later, such periods appear compressed, giving the impression that time passed quickly. Daily routines, habitual work schedules, or repetitive tasks often blur together in memory, reducing the perceived length of time.

This difference in encoding helps explain why childhood often feels prolonged in retrospect. Early life is filled with novel experiences, learning, and exploration, leading to dense memory formation. Adulthood, on the other hand, frequently involves established routines, resulting in fewer distinctive memories and a subjective acceleration of time. Thus, memory encoding directly shapes how humans reconstruct and experience the flow of time after events have passed.

2.4 Memory, Identity, and Psychological Continuity

Memory plays a central role in shaping identity. Personal narratives are constructed through remembered experiences, providing coherence to one's life story. Disruptions in memory can fracture this continuity, affecting self-perception and emotional stability.

Memory is fundamental to the formation and maintenance of personal identity. Individuals understand who they are by linking past experiences with present awareness, creating a continuous life narrative. Memories provide reference points-childhood moments, achievements, failures, relationships-that collectively shape self-concept. Without these remembered experiences, identity would lack depth and coherence, becoming fragmented and unstable.

Psychological continuity depends on the ability to recognize oneself as the same person across time despite change. People evolve in beliefs, roles, and emotions, yet memory allows them to integrate these changes into a unified story rather than experiencing them as disconnected versions of the self. Remembering past choices helps individuals understand current values; while recalling emotional experiences supports empathy toward one's earlier self.

Aspect	Role of Memory	Impact on Identity	Effect on Psychological Continuity
Personal experiences	Stores life events and emotional moments	Shapes self-concept and individuality	Connects past experiences with present self
Autobiographical narrative	Organizes memories into a life story	Provides coherence and meaning to identity	Maintains a sense of "same self" over time
Emotional memory	Retains feelings linked to events	Influences self-esteem and emotional stability	Helps integrate emotional growth across life stages
Memory disruption	Loss or distortion of recalled experiences	Causes identity confusion or fragmentation	Breaks continuity between past and present
Future self-projection	Uses past memories to imagine future roles	Supports goal setting and personal growth	Extends identity into the future

When memory is disrupted, this continuity can weaken. Conditions such as amnesia or neurodegenerative disorders often lead to confusion about identity, emotional distress, and difficulty maintaining relationships. Individuals may struggle to relate their present state to their past, resulting in a fractured sense of self. This demonstrates that identity is not fixed but actively sustained through memory.

Through memory, individuals also project identity into the future. By recalling past patterns and aspirations, they imagine who they might become and set goals accordingly. Thus, memory connects past, present, and future selves, reinforcing identity as a deeply temporal and evolving psychological construct.

Multiple Choice Questions (MCQs)

1. Which function of memory allows humans to mentally revisit past experiences?

A. Sensory encoding
B. Episodic recall
C. Perceptual filtering
D. Motor rehearsal
Answer: B

2. Which type of memory holds information for only a fraction of a second after a stimulus disappears?

A. Short-term memory
B. Long-term memory
C. Sensory memory
D. Semantic memory
Answer: C

3. Working memory is primarily responsible for:

A. Storing lifelong experiences
B. Processing and manipulating immediate information
C. Preserving emotional memories
D. Retaining unconscious knowledge
Answer: B

4. Which memory system stores general facts and knowledge without reference to time or place?

A. Episodic memory
B. Procedural memory
C. Sensory memory
D. Semantic memory
Answer: D

5. Why do repetitive routines often make time feel as if it passes quickly in hindsight?

A. They overload sensory memory
B. They reduce emotional arousal
C. They create fewer distinctive memory traces
D. They increase working memory capacity
Answer: C

Short Answer Questions

1. What is memory, and why is it essential for understanding time?
2. Define sensory memory with one example.
3. What is the role of short-term (working) memory in daily activities?
4. Differentiate between episodic memory and semantic memory.
5. How does repetitive routine affect the perception of time?
6. What is meant by psychological continuity?

Long Answer Questions

1. Explain the major types of memory and their temporal roles in human cognition.
2. Discuss how memory encoding influences the subjective experience of time.
3. Analyse the role of episodic memory in shaping personal identity.

4. Examine the effects of memory disruption on self-perception and emotional stability.
5. Describe the relationship between memory, future planning, and decision-making.
6. Evaluate how memory contributes to the continuity of the self across the lifespan.

3

Childhood and the Formation of Temporal Awareness

3.1 Early Cognitive Development and Time Understanding

In early childhood, time perception is limited to the immediate present. Young children struggle to distinguish between yesterday, today, and tomorrow. As cognitive abilities mature, children gradually understand sequences, durations, and cause-and-effect relationships over time.

In early childhood, the understanding of time is closely tied to immediate experiences rather than abstract concepts. Young children primarily live in the "now," meaning their perception of time is anchored to what is happening at the present moment. Words such as *yesterday*, *today*, and *tomorrow* are often used interchangeably by children because these terms require an ability to mentally separate events from the current situation. At this stage, time is not yet perceived as a continuous sequence but as a series of disconnected experiences.

As children grow, their cognitive development enables them to recognize patterns and sequences. Through repeated daily routines-such as waking up, going to school, eating meals, and sleeping-they begin to understand that events occur in a particular order. This sequential awareness forms the foundation for time understanding. For example, a child learns that bedtime comes after dinner or that school follows breakfast. These patterns help children predict what will happen next, even if they cannot yet measure how long something will take.

Neurological maturation plays a significant role in this progression. As the brain develops, especially areas responsible for memory, attention, and executive functioning, children become better at linking past experiences with present actions and future expectations. Memory allows them to recall previous events, while attention helps them notice changes and durations. Together, these processes enable children to grasp cause-and-effect relationships over time, such as understanding that studying earlier leads to success later.

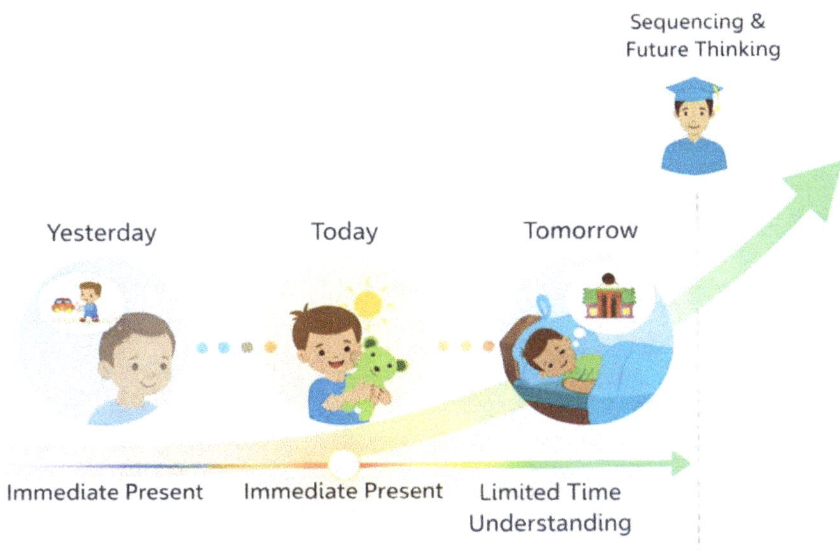

By middle childhood, children start to develop a more structured sense of time. They can estimate durations more accurately, understand calendars and clocks at a basic level, and mentally travel between past and future events. This shift reflects increasing cognitive complexity, where time is no longer just experienced but also conceptualized. Overall, early cognitive development transforms time perception from an immediate, experience-based awareness into a more organized and meaningful understanding of temporal flow.

3.2 Language, Routine, and Temporal Learning

Language plays a vital role in teaching children about time. Words related to past, present, and future help structure experiences temporally. Daily routines-such as meals, school, and sleep-also reinforce temporal patterns.

Language serves as one of the earliest tools through which children begin to understand time. Temporal words such as *before, after, soon, later*, and *tomorrow* provide labels that help children organize their experiences into meaningful sequences. When caregivers use such language consistently-by saying "we will play after lunch" or "yesterday we went to the park"-children start linking words to events. Although young children may initially misuse these terms, repeated exposure gradually helps them associate language with temporal relationships.

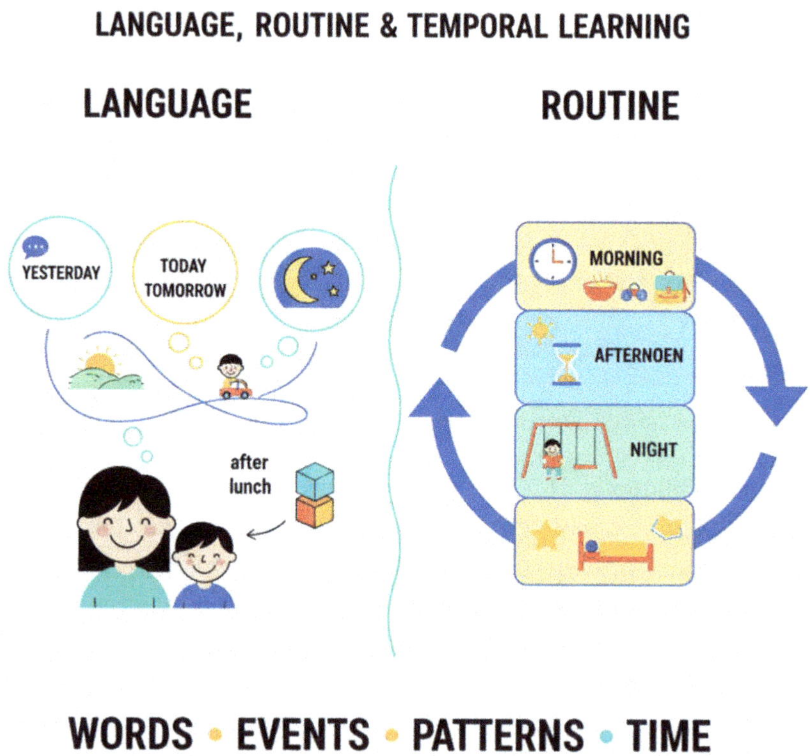

Daily routines further strengthen this learning process by offering stable and predictable patterns. Activities like waking up, eating meals, attending school, and going to bed occur in a regular order, allowing children to experience time as structured and dependable. These repeated cycles help children internalize the idea that certain events consistently follow others.

Over time, routines reduce uncertainty and make temporal sequences easier to grasp, even before children can understand clocks or calendars.

The combination of language and routine is especially powerful in shaping temporal awareness. Verbal cues embedded within daily activities-such as reminders about what comes next or reflections on what already happened-help children connect words with lived experiences. For example, hearing "first finish homework, then you can play" reinforces the idea of order, while phrases like "we will do this tomorrow" encourage children to think beyond the present moment.

Through repetition, children begin to anticipate events rather than simply react to them. Anticipation reflects a growing ability to mentally project into the future, which is a key aspect of time understanding. Gradually, children learn not only the sequence of events but also their relative timing, such as knowing that bedtime is far away in the morning but closer in the evening. Together, language, routine, and repeated interaction provide the foundation for a structured and meaningful sense of time in early

3.3 Memory Development in Childhood

Memory capacity expands rapidly during childhood. Early memories are often fragmented due to immature encoding systems. As children grow, memory becomes more organized and narrative-based.

Memory development during childhood undergoes significant qualitative and quantitative changes. In early childhood, memory capacity is limited, and memories are often fragmented or incomplete. This occurs because young children's cognitive systems for encoding, storing, and retrieving information are still immature. As a result, early memories tend to focus on isolated sensory details or emotions rather than complete events, making them difficult to recall accurately later in life.

As children grow, their memory systems become more efficient and structured. Improvements in attention, language, and executive functioning allow experiences to be encoded in a more organized manner. Instead of remembering disconnected moments, children begin to form coherent memory traces that link actions, emotions, and outcomes. Language plays a crucial role in this shift, as verbal labelling and storytelling help children organize experiences into meaningful sequences. This is why older children can describe events with a clear beginning, middle, and end.

With increasing cognitive maturity, memory also becomes narrative-based. Children learn to place experiences within a temporal framework, understanding not just what happened, but when and why it happened. This temporal organization supports learning by allowing past experiences to inform present decisions and future expectations. For example, remembering a previous mistake helps a child adjust behaviour in similar situations later. Emotional development is also strengthened, as children can reflect on past feelings and understand how emotions change over time.

Childhood memory formation has lasting implications for adulthood. The way memories are organized and stored during early years influences how individuals later reconstruct their personal history. While many early childhood memories fade-a phenomenon often called childhood amnesia-the patterns of memory development established during this period shape self-identity, emotional regulation, and autobiographical recall in later life. Thus, memory development in childhood is not only about remembering events but also about building a coherent sense of self across time.

Case Study: Memory Development and Temporal Organization in Childhood

A longitudinal observation was conducted on a child between the ages of 3 and 7 to understand how memory development evolves over time. At age 3, when asked about a recent birthday celebration, the child recalled only isolated elements such as "cake," "balloons," and "people." The child could not describe the order of events or explain when the celebration occurred. The memory appeared fragmented, with no clear beginning or sequence, reflecting early-stage encoding and limited narrative structure.

By age 5, the same child was able to recall the birthday event with greater detail and organization. The child described arriving at the venue, cutting the cake, playing games, and receiving gifts, often using temporal connectors like "first," "then," and "after that." The child could also distinguish the event as something that happened "last year," indicating an emerging ability to place experiences within a temporal framework. Emotional elements, such as feeling excited or happy, were now integrated into the memory.

At age 7, memory recall became more coherent and reflective. The child not only narrated the event in a clear sequence but also compared it with previous birthdays, noting differences and expressing preferences. For example, the child explained, "This birthday was better than the last one because my friends stayed longer." This comparison demonstrated advanced memory organization, temporal awareness, and emotional understanding.

This case study illustrates how childhood memory progresses from fragmented recall to structured, narrative-based memory. As cognitive and linguistic abilities mature, children gain the capacity to encode experiences meaningfully, place them in time, and use past memories to interpret emotions and guide future behaviour.

3.4 Imagination, Future Thinking, and Psychological Growth

Children's imagination contributes to emerging future-oriented thinking. Pretend play and storytelling allow children to simulate future scenarios and explore possibilities. This ability strengthens planning, emotional regulation, and goal formation.

Imagination plays a central role in helping children move beyond present-focused thinking toward an awareness of the future. In early childhood, imaginative abilities emerge through pretend play, storytelling, and fantasy.

When children imagine being a teacher, a doctor, or a superhero, they are not merely engaging in play; they are mentally simulating situations that do not yet exist. This capacity to envision alternative outcomes marks the beginning of future-oriented thinking.

Pretend play allows children to experiment with "what might happen" rather than only "what is happening now." For example, when a child plans a make-believe picnic or enacts a future event such as going to school, they practice sequencing actions and anticipating consequences. These imagined scenarios help children understand cause-and-effect relationships over time, strengthening their ability to plan ahead. Through repeated imaginative experiences, children learn that actions taken now can influence outcomes later.

Imagination also supports emotional regulation and psychological resilience. By envisioning future situations, children rehearse emotional responses in a safe and controlled context. A child who pretends to face a challenge-such as losing a game or resolving a conflict-can explore feelings like disappointment or anxiety without real-world consequences. This process helps children develop coping strategies and emotional flexibility, which are essential for healthy psychological growth.

As children mature, imagination becomes more structured and purposeful. They begin to imagine realistic future possibilities, such as academic success or personal achievements, and align their behaviour with these goals. This shift reflects an important step in psychological evolution: the ability to project oneself into the future and make decisions accordingly. Early development of future thinking lays the foundation for adult capacities such as long-term planning, delayed gratification, and responsible decision-making. In this way, imagination acts as a bridge between childhood play and mature psychological functioning.

Aspect of Development	Core Focus	Key Characteristics	Psychological Significance
Early Cognitive Development	Present-focused	Difficulty distinguishing	Reflects early neurological

and Time Understanding	time perception	past, present, and future; limited sense of duration and sequence	immaturity; forms the base for later temporal reasoning
Language, Routine, and Temporal Learning	Social and linguistic structuring of time	Use of temporal words (before, after, tomorrow); repetition through daily routines	Enables anticipation, prediction, and understanding of temporal order
Memory Development in Childhood	Growth of encoding and recall systems	Shift from fragmented memories to organized, narrative-based recall	Supports learning, emotional processing, and autobiographical identity
Imagination, Future Thinking, and Psychological Growth	Emergence of future-oriented cognition	Pretend play, storytelling, simulation of future scenarios	Strengthens planning, emotional regulation, goal-setting, and decision-making

Multiple Choice Questions (MCQs)

1. Why do young children struggle to distinguish between yesterday, today, and tomorrow?

a) Because they lack vocabulary skills
b) Because their perception of time is limited to the present moment
c) Because routines are absent in early childhood
d) Because memory does not develop until adolescence

Answer: b) Because their perception of time is limited to the present moment

2. How does language contribute to the development of temporal awareness in children?

a) By improving mathematical skills
b) By labelling events with past, present, and future references
c) By increasing emotional intelligence only
d) By replacing memory-based learning

Answer: b) By labelling events with past, present, and future references

3. What role do daily routines play in children's understanding of time?

a) They reduce creativity
b) They create rigid behaviour patterns
c) They reinforce predictable temporal sequences
d) They limit future thinking

Answer: c) They reinforce predictable temporal sequences

4. Why are early childhood memories often fragmented?

a) Children choose not to remember experiences
b) Emotional development is absent
c) Memory encoding systems are still immature
d) Language development stops memory formation

Answer: c) Memory encoding systems are still immature

5. How does imagination support future-oriented thinking in children?

a) By distracting children from reality
b) By encouraging emotional dependence
c) By allowing mental simulation of future scenarios
d) By reducing logical reasoning

Answer: c) By allowing mental simulation of future scenarios

Short Answer Questions

1. What is meant by present-focused time perception in early childhood?

2. Why do young children find it difficult to differentiate between yesterday, today, and tomorrow?

3. How does language help children organize experiences temporally?

4. What role do daily routines play in shaping temporal awareness?

5. Why are early childhood memories often fragmented?

6. How does imagination contribute to future-oriented thinking in children?

Long Answer Questions

1. Explain how cognitive development influences children's understanding of time and temporal sequences.

2. Discuss the combined role of language and routine in the development of temporal learning during childhood.

3. Analyse the stages of memory development in childhood and their impact on learning and emotional growth.

4. Examine the role of imagination and pretend play in fostering future thinking and planning abilities.

5. Describe how early temporal awareness contributes to psychological growth and decision-making later in life.

6. Critically evaluate the importance of childhood experiences in shaping autobiographical memory and temporal identity.

4

Adolescence, Identity, and Accelerated Time Perception

4.1 Cognitive and Emotional Transitions in Adolescence

Adolescence is marked by rapid cognitive growth and emotional volatility, both of which influence how time is experienced. As abstract thinking develops, adolescents become more aware of the past and future, often reflecting deeply on personal experiences.

Adolescence represents a crucial developmental phase in which profound changes occur in both cognition and emotion, reshaping how individuals understand themselves, others, and time itself. During this stage, the brain undergoes structural and functional maturation, particularly in areas responsible for reasoning, self-regulation, and emotional processing.

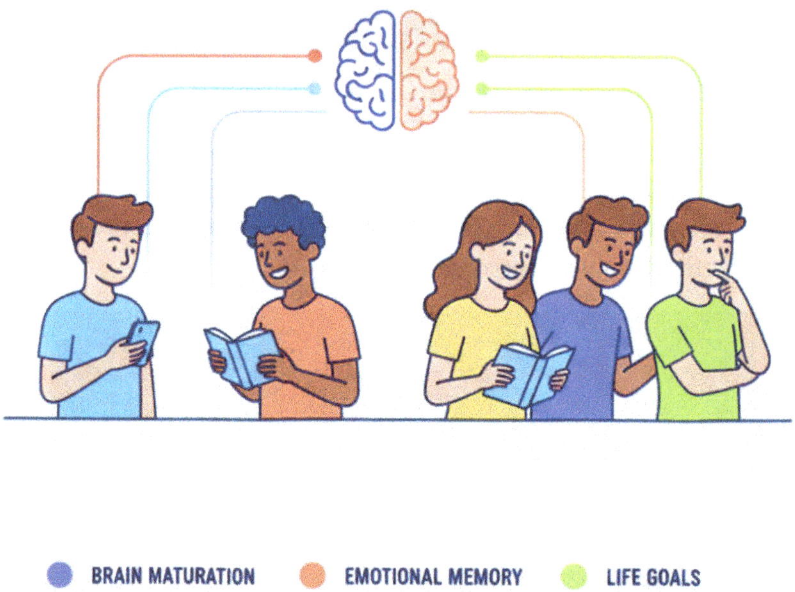

One of the most significant cognitive shifts is the emergence of abstract and reflective thinking. Adolescents move beyond concrete, present-focused thought patterns and begin to think hypothetically, imagine future possibilities, and reinterpret past experiences. This expanded mental capacity allows them to view time not merely as a sequence of events, but as a meaningful continuum connected to identity and life goals.

Emotionally, adolescence is characterized by heightened sensitivity and intensity. Fluctuations in mood, increased self-consciousness, and stronger emotional reactions are common as regulatory systems in the brain are still developing. Because emotions strongly influence perception, emotionally charged experiences-such as friendships, conflicts, achievements, or failures-often feel amplified. Moments associated with excitement, anxiety, or distress may seem to last longer or leave deeper impressions in memory. As a result, adolescents often perceive time as uneven: some periods feel overwhelming and prolonged, while others pass quickly but remain vividly remembered.

These cognitive and emotional transformations also foster a growing awareness of change and impermanence. Adolescents begin to recognize that relationships evolve, identities shift, and life stages are temporary. This realization can lead to introspection, nostalgia, and sometimes uncertainty or existential questioning. The heightened awareness of "becoming" rather than simply "being" makes time feel more significant and personal. Thus, adolescence is not only a period of rapid development but also a phase in which time is experienced more intensely, shaped by expanding thought processes and emotionally rich inner lives.

4.2 Identity Formation and Temporal Self-Awareness

During adolescence, individuals actively construct a sense of identity that connects past experiences with future aspirations. This process requires reflective memory and forward-looking imagination.

Identity formation is a central developmental task of adolescence, and it is deeply intertwined with how individuals perceive and relate to time. During this stage, adolescents begin to actively shape a coherent sense of self by integrating who they were in the past, who they are in the present, and who they hope to become in the future. Unlike childhood, where identity is largely defined by external roles and immediate experiences, adolescence introduces a more reflective and self-directed process of self-construction.

This developmental shift relies heavily on reflective memory. Adolescents increasingly revisit past experiences-such as successes, failures, relationships, and turning points-to evaluate what these moments say about their values, abilities, and personality. Memories are no longer recalled passively; instead, they are interpreted and reinterpreted to support emerging self-narratives. At the same time, adolescents develop the cognitive capacity for future-oriented thinking. They imagine potential life paths, careers, relationships, and personal goals, using these imagined futures as reference points for present decisions.

As a result, adolescents develop a strong temporal self-awareness, meaning they see themselves as existing across time rather than only in the present moment. Past experiences become lessons, and the future becomes a space of possibility and intention. This temporal orientation helps adolescents make sense of continuity and change in their identity, even as they experiment with different roles, beliefs, and behaviours.

In this context, time functions as a psychological framework for self-definition. Rather than viewing time simply as a chronological flow of events, adolescents use it to organize their identity-linking memories, present actions, and future aspirations into a meaningful personal story. This ability to position the self within time is essential for developing purpose, autonomy, and a stable sense of who one is becoming.

4.3 Novelty, Memory Density, and the Speed of Time

Adolescent life is rich in new experiences-social relationships, emotional milestones, and cognitive challenges. These novel events generate dense memory encoding, making this period feel expansive in hindsight.

Adolescence is a life stage characterized by a high concentration of first-time experiences, ranging from new social roles and emotional relationships to intellectual and personal challenges. These experiences demand heightened attention and emotional involvement, which significantly influences how memories are formed. When events are novel, the brain allocates more cognitive resources to processing them, resulting in richer and more detailed memory encoding. As a result, adolescence becomes a period of high memory density, meaning that many distinct, vivid memories are stored within a relatively short span of chronological time.

This dense accumulation of memories affects how time is perceived in retrospect. When adolescents-or adults looking back-recall this phase of life, the abundance of memorable moments creates the impression that adolescence lasted longer than it actually did. Each memory acts as a psychological marker, expanding the perceived duration of this life stage. This is why adolescence often feels expansive and eventful when remembered later, compared to more routine periods of adulthood that generate fewer distinct memories.

Aspect	Description
Past Orientation	Adolescents reflect on past experiences to evaluate personal values, strengths, mistakes, and formative events that shape their emerging identity.
Present Self	Current thoughts, emotions, and behaviours are examined in relation to personal beliefs and social roles, helping adolescents understand who they are now.
Future Orientation	Imagination and goal-setting allow adolescents to envision possible futures, including careers, relationships, and life aspirations.
Temporal Integration	Past memories and future goals are psychologically connected, creating a coherent sense of self across time.
Role of Time	Time functions as a tool for self-definition, enabling adolescents to construct a personal life narrative rather than viewing life as isolated events.
Outcome	Development of temporal self-awareness, purpose, and a more stable yet evolving identity.

Interestingly, this retrospective expansion contrasts with how time is often experienced in the moment. During emotionally engaging or absorbing activities, adolescents may feel that time passes quickly. Intense focus on social interactions, passions, or emotional experiences can reduce awareness of time passing, creating a sense of acceleration. This phenomenon occurs because attention is directed outward or inward toward the experience itself rather than toward monitoring time.

Together, these opposing perceptions create a dual experience of time in adolescence. While individual moments may feel fleeting as they unfold, the overall period feels intense and prolonged when recalled later. This combination of accelerated present-time experience and expanded retrospective memory explains why adolescence is commonly described as both deeply impactful and surprisingly brief.

4.4 Risk-Taking and Future Discounting

Adolescents tend to prioritize immediate rewards over long-term consequences; a phenomenon linked to ongoing neurological development. This temporal bias affects decision-making, leading to risk-taking behaviours.

Risk-taking during adolescence is closely tied to how young individuals perceive and evaluate time. At this developmental stage, adolescents often place greater value on immediate rewards than on outcomes that lie further in the future. This tendency, known as **future discounting**, reflects the way the developing brain weighs present satisfaction against delayed consequences. Because long-term outcomes feel psychologically distant, they carry less motivational force in adolescent decision-making.

Neurological development plays a central role in this temporal bias. Brain regions associated with reward sensitivity and emotional arousal mature earlier than those responsible for impulse control, planning, and long-term evaluation. As a result, adolescents may be highly responsive to immediate incentives such as peer approval, excitement, or pleasure, while having a limited capacity to fully anticipate future risks or negative consequences. This imbalance can lead to behaviours such as reckless driving, substance experimentation, or impulsive social decisions.

Importantly, this pattern does not indicate a lack of intelligence or awareness. Many adolescents understand potential risks at a factual level, yet the emotional pull of the present moment often outweighs abstract future considerations. Their ability to project themselves into the future and emotionally connect with long-term outcomes is still developing. Consequently, decisions are often guided by how rewarding or meaningful an action feels now rather than by its future impact.

Over time, as cognitive control and executive functioning improve, adolescents gain a stronger capacity to integrate future consequences into present choices. Maturation of planning, self-regulation, and reflective thinking allows individuals to balance immediate desires with long-term goals more effectively. This developmental shift leads to greater temporal balance, enabling more deliberate and purposeful decision-making as adolescence transitions into adulthood.

Multiple Choice Questions (MCQs)

1. Why does adolescence often involve heightened emotional intensity that affects time perception?

A. Because memory capacity decreases during adolescence
B. Because emotional regulation systems mature faster than cognitive systems
C. Because emotional experiences strongly influence attention and perception
D. Because adolescents lack awareness of past and future

Correct Answer: C

2. What role does identity formation play in adolescents' perception of time?

A. It reduces attention to future planning
B. It disconnects past experiences from present behaviour
C. It links past memories with future aspirations
D. It limits self-reflection

Correct Answer: C

3. Why does adolescence feel expansive in hindsight despite feeling fast in the moment?

A. Routine activities slow time perception
B. High memory density from novel experiences expands retrospective time
C. Adolescents overestimate time intervals
D. Emotional detachment increases memory recall

Correct Answer: B

4. What is meant by future discounting in adolescent decision-making?

A. Ignoring past experiences when making choices
B. Overestimating long-term risks
C. Valuing immediate rewards more than future outcomes
D. Planning excessively for adulthood

Correct Answer: C

5. How does cognitive maturation influence temporal balance in late adolescence?

A. It eliminates emotional influence on decisions
B. It increases impulsivity
C. It strengthens the ability to integrate future goals with present actions
D. It reduces self-awareness

Correct Answer: C

Short Answer Questions

1. What cognitive changes during adolescence influence the perception of time?
2. How does emotional intensity affect adolescents' experience of time?
3. Define temporal self-awareness in the context of identity formation.
4. What is meant by memory density, and why is it high during adolescence?
5. Explain future discounting in adolescent decision-making.
6. Why does adolescence often feel brief when experienced but long in retrospect?

Long Answer Questions

1. Discuss how cognitive and emotional transitions during adolescence reshape the subjective experience of time.
2. Explain the role of identity formation in linking past experiences with future aspirations during adolescence.
3. Analyse the relationship between novelty, memory encoding, and retrospective time perception in adolescence.
4. Examine the neurological basis of risk-taking behaviour and future discounting in adolescents.
5. Describe how emotional engagement can simultaneously accelerate present-time perception and intensify long-term memory formation.
6. Evaluate how improved cognitive control over time leads to a better balance between present desires and future goals in late adolescence.

5

Adulthood, Routine, and the Compression of Time

5.1 Stability, Responsibility, and Temporal Structuring

Adulthood introduces stable roles and responsibilities that structure daily life. Work schedules, family obligations, and social norms impose regularity on time use. While this structure enhances efficiency, it reduces variability in experiences.

Adulthood is marked by the adoption of enduring social roles and long-term responsibilities that bring order and predictability to everyday life. Professional commitments, household duties, and societal expectations collectively organize time into fixed patterns. Regular work hours, recurring routines, and scheduled obligations create a structured temporal framework that helps individuals manage multiple demands efficiently. This organization of time supports goal attainment, reliability, and social coordination, making adult life more stable and functionally effective.

However, this same stability can subtly reshape how time is experienced psychologically. When daily activities follow familiar and repetitive patterns, fewer events stand out as distinct or memorable. Novelty-an important factor in how the brain encodes experiences-becomes less frequent. As a result, individual days may feel shorter or less differentiated when recalled, even though they are filled with activity. Over weeks and months, this repetition can cause time to feel as though it is moving more quickly in retrospect, because the mind has fewer unique reference points to anchor memories.

Responsibility also influences attention and emotional focus. Adults often concentrate on future-oriented goals such as career advancement, financial security, or family well-being. This forward-looking mindset shifts attention away from the present moment, making time feel compressed as individuals move quickly from one obligation to the next. While this temporal structuring promotes productivity and long-term planning, it can diminish subjective richness if not balanced with variety and reflective pauses.

Thus, adulthood's stability provides essential structure and reliability, but it also transforms time perception. Time becomes organized, efficient, and purpose-driven, yet potentially less vivid. Understanding these dynamic highlights the importance of consciously introducing variation, reflection, and meaningful experiences to preserve a sense of temporal depth and personal fulfilment within adult life.

5.2 Routine, Habit Formation, and Memory Sparsity

Repetition leads to habit formation, allowing tasks to be performed with minimal conscious attention. While efficient, habitual behaviour produces fewer distinctive memories. When reflecting on long periods dominated by routine, individuals may feel that time has passed quickly.

Routine is a defining feature of adult life, emerging as repeated behaviours gradually transform into habits. Through habit formation, frequently performed actions-such as commuting, work-related tasks, or household activities-become automatic and require little conscious thought. This automation is cognitively efficient, freeing mental resources for complex decision-making and problem-solving. By reducing the need for constant attention, habits enable individuals to function smoothly in demanding environments.

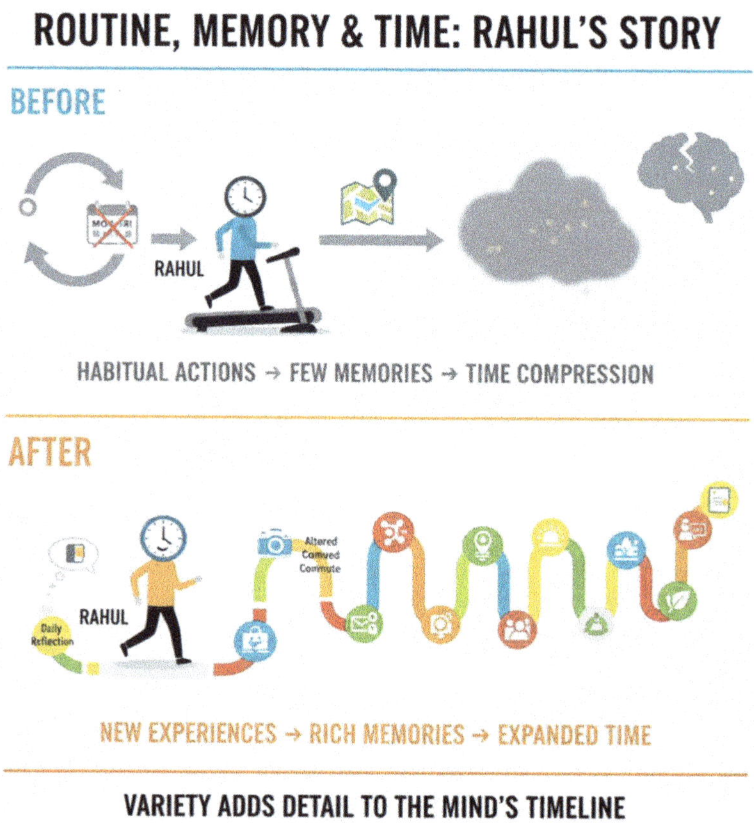

However, this efficiency comes with a psychological trade-off in how time is remembered. When actions are repeated in similar contexts, the brain expends less effort encoding them as unique events. Memory formation thrives on novelty and emotional engagement; routine activities, by contrast, generate fewer distinctive memory markers. As a result, days filled with habitual behaviours may be experienced as full and busy in the moment yet appear compressed or blurred when recalled later.

This phenomenon explains why extended periods dominated by routine can feel as though they passed rapidly in retrospect. The perception is not caused by a lack of experiences, but by a lack of variation among them. Without clear mental boundaries separating one day from another, memories merge into a generalized impression rather than a sequence of vivid moments. Time, therefore, seems to accelerate when viewed from a distance.

Understanding the relationship between habit and memory highlights an important aspect of subjective time perception. While routines are essential for stability and efficiency, consciously introducing small changes, reflective moments, or novel experiences can enrich memory encoding. Such variation helps create meaningful distinctions in time, preserving a fuller and more textured sense of lived experience even within structured and habitual adult life.

Case Study: Routine, Habit Formation, and the Experience of Accelerated Time

Background:

Rahul, a 38-year-old software engineer living in Bengaluru, has followed a highly structured routine for nearly eight years. His weekdays are predictable: waking at the same time, commuting along the same route, working fixed hours, returning home, having dinner, and spending the evening watching television or browsing his phone. His weekends are similarly patterned, involving household chores and family visits. Rahul reports feeling constantly busy and productive, yet he often expresses surprise at how quickly months and even years seem to pass.

Observation:

When Rahul reflects on the previous year, he struggles to recall specific events or moments that clearly differentiate one month from another. Aside from major milestones-such as a project deadline or a family function-most days feel indistinguishable in memory. Despite having worked consistently and accomplished professional goals, the year feels "compressed," as though it disappeared rapidly.

Psychological Explanation:
Rahul's experience illustrates the relationship between routine, habit formation, and memory sparsity. Because his daily activities are repetitive, many of his behaviours are governed by habits rather than conscious attention. Habitual actions require minimal cognitive effort, which reduces the depth of memory encoding. As a result, fewer distinctive memory traces are formed, even though his days are objectively full of activity. When the brain looks back on this period, it finds limited memorable landmarks, leading to the impression that time has passed unusually fast.

Change and Outcome:
During a six-month period, Rahul deliberately introduced small variations into his routine. He joined a weekend photography group, altered his commute occasionally, and set aside time each evening to reflect briefly on his day. When later asked to recall this period, he described it as feeling longer and more vivid. He could easily identify specific moments, experiences, and emotions associated with those months.

5.3 Goal Orientation and Future Planning

Adults often focus heavily on future outcomes such as career advancement, financial security, and family stability. This purposeful mindset shifts attention away from the present moment. When time is viewed primarily as a resource to be managed, subjective experience becomes secondary.

In adulthood, life is increasingly guided by long-term objectives that provide direction and purpose. Goals related to professional growth, economic stability, and family responsibilities shape daily decisions and priorities. This forward-looking orientation encourages planning, evaluation, and constant assessment of progress. Time, in this context, is often treated as a limited resource that must be allocated efficiently to achieve desired outcomes. Such a mindset supports discipline, persistence, and strategic thinking, all of which are essential for sustained success.

At the same time, an intense focus on future goals subtly alters subjective time perception. Attention is frequently directed toward what lies ahead rather than what is occurring in the present moment. When individuals move from one task to the next with an emphasis on completion and results, experiences are often processed instrumentally rather than reflectively. Moments become steps in a larger plan instead of experiences to be fully absorbed. This reduces emotional and sensory engagement with the present, which plays a key role in how richly time is experienced.

As a consequence, time may feel as though it is passing quickly. When the present is overshadowed by anticipation of future outcomes, fewer moments are deeply encoded in memory. Looking back, long stretches of life appear condensed, not because they lacked meaning or effort, but because they were experienced through the lens of efficiency rather than awareness. Days become units of progress rather than lived experiences.

Thus, goal orientation and future planning, while essential for adult functioning, contribute to the sensation of accelerated time. Balancing long-term planning with mindful attention to the present can help preserve subjective depth, allowing time to feel not only productive, but also personally meaningful and experientially rich.

5.4 Reclaiming Psychological Time

Despite temporal compression, adults can alter time perception through mindful engagement and novelty. Learning new skills, traveling, or reflecting on experiences increases memory richness. Conscious engagement with the present slows subjective time and enhances life satisfaction.

Although adulthood is often associated with a sense of time speeding up, psychological time is not permanently compressed. Adults retain the capacity to reshape how time is experienced by changing how they engage with their daily lives. Subjective time perception is strongly influenced by attention, emotion, and memory formation, all of which remain flexible across the lifespan. This means that even within structured and responsibility-driven routines, individuals can actively reclaim a richer sense of lived time.

One powerful way to do this is through mindful engagement with the present moment. When attention is deliberately focused on ongoing experiences-such as conversations, sensory details, or emotions-those moments are processed more deeply. Mindfulness interrupts automatic, goal-driven behaviour and restores awareness to the "now." This heightened presence makes moments feel fuller and more extended, counteracting the tendency for days to blur together. Over time, such engagement enhances emotional connection to experiences and supports greater well-being.

Novelty also plays a crucial role in expanding psychological time. Learning a new skill, exploring unfamiliar environments, or engaging in creative activities introduces variation into daily life. Novel experiences demand greater cognitive processing, leading to stronger and more detailed memory encoding. When individuals later reflect on these periods, the abundance of distinct memories makes time feel longer and more substantial in retrospect. Importantly, novelty does not require dramatic life changes; even small deviations from routine can significantly enrich memory.

Reflection further strengthens this process. Taking time to think about experiences-through journaling, discussion, or quiet contemplation-helps consolidate memories and assign meaning to events. Reflection transforms passing moments into coherent narratives, reinforcing a sense of continuity and personal growth. Together, mindfulness, novelty, and reflection demonstrate that time perception in adulthood is not rigid or predetermined. By consciously shaping how experiences are lived and remembered, adults can slow subjective time, deepen life satisfaction, and reclaim a sense of temporal richness within everyday life.

Dimension	Everyday Condition	Conscious Intervention	Effect on Memory Encoding	Impact on Time Perception
Attention	Automatic, task-driven focus	Mindful engagement with present activities	Deeper, more detailed memories	Time feels slower and fuller
Experience Variety	Repetitive routines	Introduction of novelty (learning, travel, new hobbies)	Increased memory distinctiveness	Past periods feel longer in retrospect
Cognitive Processing	Habitual, low-effort processing	Active learning and skill acquisition	Richer cognitive and emotional traces	Reduced sense of time compression
Reflection	Little recall or evaluation	Journaling, reflection, or discussion	Stronger consolidation of experiences	Greater temporal depth and continuity
Emotional Engagement	Neutral or muted emotions	Meaningful and emotionally engaging activities	Emotionally tagged memories	Enhanced life satisfaction and vivid time experience

Multiple-Choice Questions (MCQs)

1. Why does time often feel as though it passes more quickly during adulthood?

a) Adults have fewer responsibilities

b) Daily life becomes less emotionally intense

c) Routine reduces memory distinctiveness

d) Biological aging shortens objective time

Answer: c) Routine reduces memory distinctiveness

2. How does habit formation influence subjective time perception?

a) It increases emotional arousal in daily tasks

b) It requires more conscious attention

c) It leads to richer memory encoding

d) It reduces conscious processing and memory formation

Answer: d) It reduces conscious processing and memory formation

3. What role does goal orientation play in the perception of time in adulthood?

a) It increases awareness of present experiences

b) It shifts attention toward past memories

c) It emphasizes present-moment enjoyment

d) It directs attention toward future outcomes

Answer: d) It directs attention toward future outcomes

4. Which factor most strongly contributes to the feeling that long periods of adult life pass quickly in retrospect?

a) Physical fatigue

b) Lack of objective experiences

c) Reduced emotional intelligence

d) Fewer distinctive memory markers

Answer: d) Fewer distinctive memory markers

5. Which strategy can help adults reclaim a richer sense of psychological time?

a) Increasing multitasking

b) Eliminating long-term goals

c) Engaging in mindfulness and novel experiences

d) Strictly maintaining routines

Answer: c) Engaging in mindfulness and novel experiences

Short Answer Questions

1. What is meant by *temporal compression* in adulthood?
2. How does routine contribute to reduced memory distinctiveness?
3. Why does habit formation lower conscious attention in daily tasks?
4. In what way does purposeful thinking shift attention away from the present?
5. How does memory sparsity affect retrospective time perception?
6. What role does mindfulness play in reclaiming psychological time?

Long Answer Questions

1. Explain how stability and responsibility structure adult life and alter subjective time perception.
2. Discuss the relationship between routine, habit formation, and memory sparsity, with suitable examples.
3. Analyse how a future-oriented, goal-driven mindset contributes to the sensation of accelerated time in adulthood.
4. Examine the psychological mechanisms that cause long periods of routine-filled adult life to feel compressed in retrospect.
5. Describe strategies adults can use to reclaim psychological time and enhance memory richness.
6. Critically evaluate whether time perception in adulthood is fixed or flexible, supporting your answer with psychological reasoning.

6

Aging, Memory Transformation, and Psychological Adaptation

6.1 Cognitive Aging and Changes in Time Awareness

As individuals age, certain cognitive functions such as processing speed and working memory may decline, affecting time estimation. Older adults may perceive time as moving faster due to reduced novelty and changes in attention.

Cognitive aging brings gradual changes in how individuals process, interpret, and experience time. As people grow older, certain cognitive abilities-particularly processing speed and working memory-tend to slow. These functions play an important role in tracking durations, sequencing events, and updating ongoing experiences. When mental processing becomes less rapid, fewer temporal markers are consciously registered in daily life, which can subtly alter how the passage of time is perceived.

One commonly reported experience among older adults is the feeling that time moves more quickly. This perception is not simply the result of cognitive decline, but rather a shift in how experiences are structured and attended to. With age, daily life often becomes more predictable, with fewer novel or emotionally intense events compared to earlier life stages. Novelty is a key factor in creating distinct memory traces. When fewer new experiences are encoded, long stretches of time may appear compressed in retrospect, giving the impression that months or years have passed rapidly.

Attention also plays a central role in time awareness. Older adults may allocate attention more selectively, focusing on meaningful or emotionally relevant experiences rather than constantly monitoring the flow of time. This reduced temporal monitoring can make time feel as though it is passing faster, even though moment-to-moment experiences remain rich and significant.

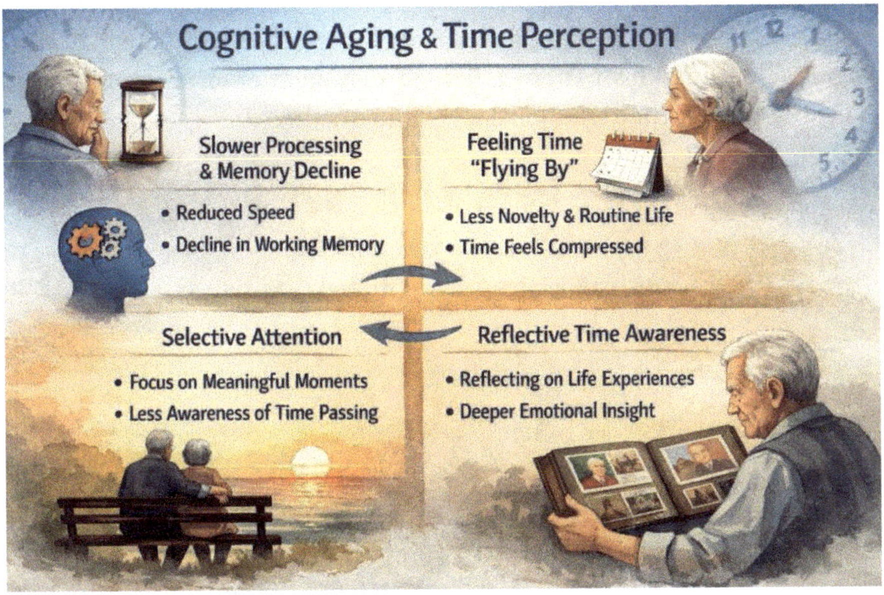

Importantly, cognitive aging does not imply a loss of psychological depth or temporal understanding. In many cases, time awareness becomes more reflective and emotionally layered. Older individuals often interpret time through the lens of accumulated life experience, integrating past memories with present meaning and future considerations. This reflective orientation allows time to be experienced less as a sequence of measured units and more as a narrative shaped by values, relationships, and personal significance. Thus, while the subjective speed of time may increase with age, its emotional and psychological complexity often deepens.

6.2 Memory Recall, Reminiscence, and Life Review

Later life is characterized by increased reminiscence, where individuals frequently revisit past experiences. Long-term memories, especially emotionally significant ones, remain vivid. This reflective engagement supports emotional regulation and meaning-making.

In later life, memory processes often shift from acquiring new information toward reflecting on past experiences. This stage is marked by an increased tendency for reminiscence, where individuals naturally revisit earlier life events, relationships, achievements, and challenges. Rather than indicating cognitive decline, this pattern reflects a reorientation of memory toward meaning, identity, and emotional understanding.

Long-term memories-particularly those tied to strong emotions-tend to remain relatively stable across aging. Experiences involving love, loss, success, or personal transformation are often vividly recalled because emotional significance strengthens memory encoding and retrieval. These memories may surface spontaneously or through deliberate reflection, serving as anchors that connect the present self to earlier life stages.

Reminiscence plays an important role in emotional regulation. By revisiting past experiences, older adults are able to reinterpret difficult events, reframe regrets, and appreciate personal growth over time. This reflective process can reduce emotional distress, enhance acceptance, and foster a sense of psychological balance. Positive memories, in particular, contribute to well-being by reinforcing feelings of continuity, belonging, and self-worth.

Life review goes beyond casual remembering and involves actively organizing one's experiences into a coherent narrative. Through this process, individuals integrate successes and failures into a unified understanding of their life journey. Constructing such a narrative helps clarify personal values, resolve unresolved conflicts, and derive meaning from both positive and adverse experiences.

Overall, memory recall and reminiscence in later life support a deeper sense of identity and purpose. By weaving together past experiences into a meaningful story, individuals strengthen their sense of continuity across time. This reflective engagement allows the past to inform the present, contributing to emotional maturity, self-understanding, and a more integrated perception of one's life as a whole.

6.3 Emotional Regulation and Temporal Perspective

Older adults often exhibit improved emotional regulation compared to younger individuals. With a shorter perceived future horizon, priorities shift toward meaningful relationships and experiences. This temporal perspective encourages present-focused satisfaction rather than future-oriented striving.

As individuals grow older, emotional regulation often improves despite age-related changes in cognitive or physical functioning. Older adults tend to manage emotions more effectively, experiencing fewer extreme emotional fluctuations and recovering more quickly from negative experiences. This enhanced regulation is intricately linked to changes in temporal perspective-that is, how individuals perceive and value the time they have ahead of them.

With advancing age, the future is often perceived as more limited. Rather than triggering anxiety, this shortened future horizon frequently leads to a reorganization of priorities. Older adults become more selective about how they invest their time and emotional energy. Goals cantered on long-term achievement, competition, or status gradually give way to goals focused on emotional meaning, connection, and personal fulfilment.

This shift encourages greater attention to the present moment. Older individuals are more likely to seek satisfaction in everyday experiences, such as meaningful conversations, shared routines, or quiet reflection. Because time is seen as valuable and finite, it is used more intentionally. Emotional experiences are chosen carefully, and situations that generate unnecessary stress or conflict are often avoided.

As a result, time is no longer evaluated primarily in terms of how much remains, but in terms of its quality. Moments are appreciated for their depth, emotional richness, and personal significance rather than their role in achieving future outcomes. This perspective supports well-being by aligning emotional goals with realistic temporal awareness. Ultimately, emotional regulation in later life reflects a mature integration of time, meaning, and emotion, allowing individuals to experience satisfaction through presence, acceptance, and meaningful engagement.

6.4 Adaptation, Wisdom, and Psychological Resilience

Psychological adaptation in aging involves accepting temporal limitations while drawing on accumulated experience. Wisdom emerges from integrating knowledge across time, enabling balanced decision-making.

Aging is accompanied not only by biological and cognitive changes, but also by powerful psychological adaptations that shape how individuals understand time, self, and life experiences. One of the most significant aspects of this stage is the ability to accept temporal limitations. Rather than resisting the reality of aging, many individuals gradually come to terms with finite time horizons, adjusting goals and expectations in ways that preserve emotional balance and psychological well-being.

This adaptation is supported by accumulated life experience. Over decades, individuals encounter success, failure, loss, and recovery, building a rich internal repository of knowledge. Wisdom emerges from the ability to integrate these experiences across time, recognizing patterns in human behaviour, consequences of choices, and the transient nature of circumstances. Unlike raw intelligence or speed of processing, wisdom relies on reflection, emotional insight, and contextual understanding, allowing older adults to make more balanced and measured decisions.

Psychological resilience is another hallmark of aging. While later life often involves change-such as retirement, health challenges, or the loss of loved ones-many older adults demonstrate a strong capacity to cope. This resilience is rooted in cognitive and emotional reframing. Instead of viewing loss as purely negative, aging individuals are more likely to interpret change as a natural part of life's progression. Past experiences of overcoming adversity provide reassurance that adaptation is possible, even in difficult circumstances.

Dimension	Description	Impact on Time Perception	Psychological Outcome
Psychological adaptation	Acceptance of age-related changes and temporal limitations	Time is viewed as finite but meaningful	Reduced anxiety and greater emotional balance
Accumulated experience	Integration of life events across different life stages	Past, present, and future are seen as interconnected	Development of insight and perspective
Wisdom	Ability to apply knowledge with emotional and contextual understanding	Time is interpreted through reflection rather than urgency	Balanced and thoughtful decision-making
Emotional resilience	Capacity to cope with loss, change, and uncertainty	Setbacks are framed as part of life's flow	Greater coping strength and stability
Reframing of loss	Viewing decline or loss as natural progression	Time is accepted rather than resisted	Increased acceptance and inner peace
Self-concept transformation	Shift from achievement-based identity to meaning-based identity	Time is valued for depth and coherence	Stronger sense of purpose and continuity

Importantly, this stage of life does not represent a simple decline in mental or emotional functioning. Rather, it reflects a transformation in how time and identity are understood. Time is no longer seen as something to be conquered or maximized, but as a meaningful dimension through which life is interpreted. The self becomes less focused on achievement and more oriented toward coherence, acceptance, and understanding. Through adaptation, wisdom, and resilience, aging reveals a mature psychological relationship with time-one that emphasizes meaning, continuity, and inner stability.

Multiple Choice Questions (MCQs)

1. Which cognitive change most commonly influences time estimation in older adults?

A. Increase in sensory sensitivity
B. Decline in processing speed and working memory
C. Expansion of attentional capacity
D. Heightened novelty-seeking behaviour
Answer: B

2. Why do many older adults report that time seems to pass more quickly?

A. Biological clocks accelerate with age
B. Reduced emotional engagement with life
C. Fewer novel experiences and selective attention to time
D. Complete loss of temporal awareness
Answer: C

3. What role does reminiscence play in later adulthood?

A. It increases confusion between past and present
B. It weakens emotional regulation
C. It supports meaning-making and emotional balance
D. It replaces the need for present experiences
Answer: C

4. How does temporal perspective change emotional priorities in older adults?

A. Focus shifts toward long-term achievement and competition
B. Emphasis moves to emotionally meaningful relationships and experiences
C. Future planning becomes the dominant concern
D. Emotional goals become less important overall
Answer: B

5. Which statement best describes psychological resilience in aging?

A. Avoiding all reminders of loss or change
B. Experiencing fewer life challenges than earlier stages
C. Reframing loss and change as part of life's progression
D. Eliminating emotional responses to aging
Answer: C

Short Answer Questions

1. What cognitive changes in aging influence subjective time perception?
2. Define reminiscence and explain its significance in later adulthood.
3. How does reduced novelty affect the perception of time in older adults?
4. What is meant by a shortened future time horizon in aging?
5. How does emotional regulation improve with age?
6. What role does accumulate life experience play in psychological adaptation?

Long Answer Questions

1. Discuss how cognitive aging affects time awareness and subjective time perception in later life.

2. Explain the processes of reminiscence and life review and their contribution to emotional well-being in older adults.
3. Analyse the relationship between temporal perspective and emotional regulation during aging.
4. Describe how wisdom develops through the integration of past experiences across the lifespan.
5. Examine psychological resilience in aging, focusing on adaptation to loss, change, and temporal limitations.
6. Critically evaluate the idea that aging represents psychological transformation rather than cognitive decline.

7

The Neuroscience of Time and Memory Across the Lifespan

7.1 Brain Systems Involved in Time Perception

Time perception is supported by distributed neural networks rather than a single "time centre" in the brain. Regions such as the prefrontal cortex contribute to planning and future thinking, while subcortical structures assist in interval estimation.

Human perception of time does not arise from a single, dedicated "clock" within the brain. Instead, it emerges from the coordinated activity of multiple neural systems that work together to track duration, sequence events, and anticipate future outcomes. This distributed arrangement allows time perception to flexibly adapt to different tasks, emotional states, and stages of life.

The prefrontal cortex plays a central role in higher-order temporal functions such as planning, goal setting, and imagining future scenarios. When individuals estimate how long a task will take or reflect on past experiences in relation to future goals, this region helps organize time into meaningful cognitive frameworks. Its involvement explains why time perception is intricately linked to decision-making and self-control rather than being a purely sensory experience.

Subcortical structures contribute more directly to measuring short intervals and rhythmic patterns. These regions support internal timing mechanisms that allow people to judge seconds and minutes, coordinate movements, and maintain temporal consistency during repetitive actions. Together with the cerebellum-which refines timing through prediction and error correction-these systems enable precise estimation and synchronization with the external world.

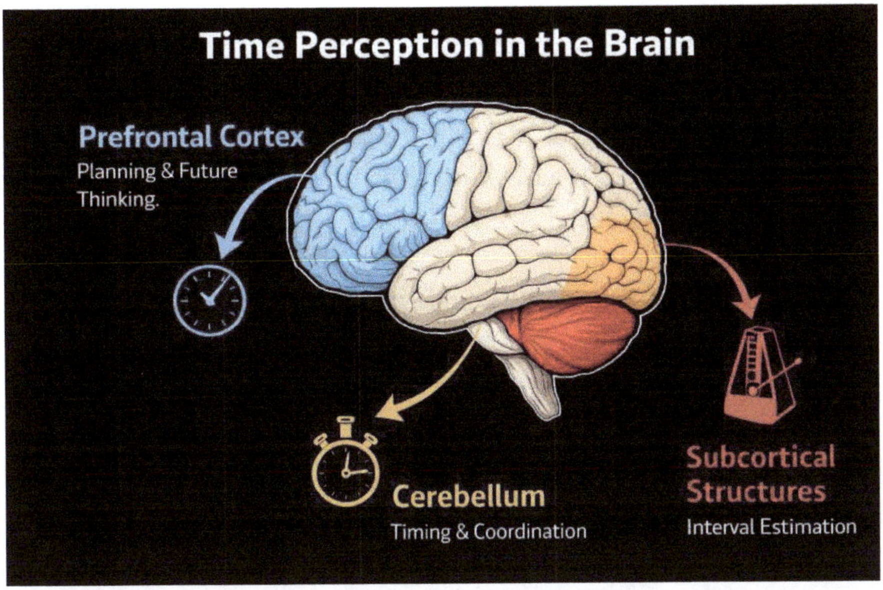

Importantly, the efficiency and coordination of these brain systems evolve across the lifespan. In childhood, neural networks responsible for timing are still developing, leading to difficulties in accurately judging duration or waiting for delayed outcomes. As the brain matures, repeated experience and neural refinement strengthen connectivity among timing-related regions, resulting in more stable and accurate internal clocks in adulthood. With aging, some aspects of this coordination may decline, subtly altering how time is experienced without eliminating the capacity for temporal understanding.

Overall, time perception reflects the dynamic integration of cognitive control, memory, and neural timing systems. Its development across life illustrates how biological maturation and experience jointly shape the way humans understand and live within time.

7.2 Memory Circuits and Lifespan Changes

Memory formation and retrieval depend on interconnected brain circuits that evolve over time. In early life, these circuits prioritize learning and adaptability, while in adulthood they emphasize efficiency and stability.

Human memory is supported by a network of interconnected brain circuits rather than a single storage site. Key regions involved in memory formation and retrieval interact dynamically, and their roles shift as individuals move through different stages of life. These changes influence not only how memories are formed but also which experiences remain most vivid over time.

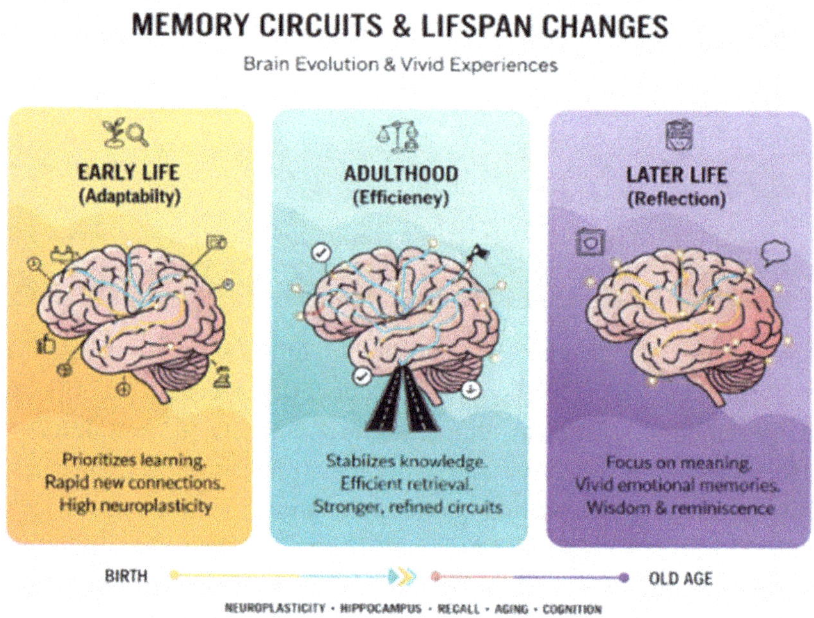

During early life, memory circuits are highly plastic and oriented toward learning and adaptation. The brain prioritizes encoding new information, skills, and social experiences, allowing children and adolescents to rapidly absorb knowledge from their environments. Neural connections are flexible, and memory systems focus on exploration and integration, even if recall is sometimes inconsistent or fragmented. This phase supports identity development and cognitive growth rather than long-term efficiency.

In adulthood, memory circuits gradually shift toward stability and optimization. The brain becomes more selective about what it encodes, often favouring information that is meaningful, goal-relevant, or emotionally significant. While the rate of forming entirely new memories may slow compared to childhood, retrieval becomes more organized and dependable. Experiences are more easily linked to existing knowledge, allowing adults to use memory strategically for problem-solving, planning, and decision-making.

In later life, a distinct pattern emerges: the ability to retrieve long-term memories often remains relatively strong, even as the formation of new episodic memories becomes more effortful. This shift reflects changes in neural encoding and consolidation rather than a simple loss of memory capacity. A well-known illustration of this pattern is the *reminiscence bump*, in which older adults recall events from adolescence and early adulthood with exceptional clarity. These memories were encoded during a period of intense novelty, emotional significance, and identity formation, making them more durable over time.

Overall, lifespan changes in memory circuits demonstrate that memory is not static but adaptive. The brain continually reshapes how experiences are stored and accessed, reflecting developmental priorities at each life stage. This evolving balance between learning, efficiency, and preservation explains why certain memories endure while others fade, shaping how individuals understand their past and experience the passage of time.

7.3 Neuroplasticity and Temporal Adaptation

Neuroplasticity-the brain's ability to reorganize itself-plays a key role in adapting to temporal demands. Although plasticity is highest in childhood, it persists throughout life.

Neuroplasticity refers to the brain's capacity to modify its structure and functional organization in response to experience, learning, and environmental demands. This adaptive property is fundamental to how humans adjust not only to new skills and information but also to changing perceptions of time. Because time perception depends on attention, memory, and prediction, plastic changes in these systems directly influence how temporal experiences are constructed.

In childhood, neuroplasticity is especially pronounced, allowing rapid formation and reorganization of neural connections. During this period, the brain readily adapts to new temporal patterns, such as learning routines, sequencing actions, and understanding duration. These early adaptations establish foundational timing skills that support later cognitive development. However, plasticity does not disappear after childhood; rather, it becomes more selective and experience-driven across adulthood.

In adults, engaging in cognitively demanding activities can reshape neural networks involved in timing and memory. Learning a new language, for example, requires tracking rhythms, sequences, and temporal structures in speech, while musical training involves precise timing and synchronization. Such activities strengthen attentional control and working memory, often leading individuals to report greater temporal awareness and improved estimation of duration. These changes reflect ongoing neural refinement rather than the creation of entirely new systems.

Even in later life, the brain retains a meaningful capacity for adaptation. Case studies of older adults involved in cognitive training-such as memory exercises, problem-solving tasks, or attention-focused programs-show improvements in mental flexibility and recall. Participants often describe a heightened sense of presence and a slower, more deliberate experience of time. These outcomes suggest that late-life neuroplasticity can counteract some age-related declines by enhancing how temporal information is processed and integrated.

Overall, neuroplasticity enables continuous temporal adaptation across the lifespan. By reshaping attention, memory, and predictive mechanisms, the brain remains capable of adjusting how time is experienced. This enduring flexibility highlights that temporal awareness is not fixed by age but can be influenced through active engagement, learning, and sustained cognitive stimulation.

7.4 Neurological Disorders and Distorted Time Experience

Certain neurological conditions profoundly affect time perception and memory. Individuals with Parkinson's disease, for instance, may struggle with time estimation due to disrupted neural timing mechanisms. Similarly, memory disorders can fragment the sense of past and future, confining individuals to a perpetual present.

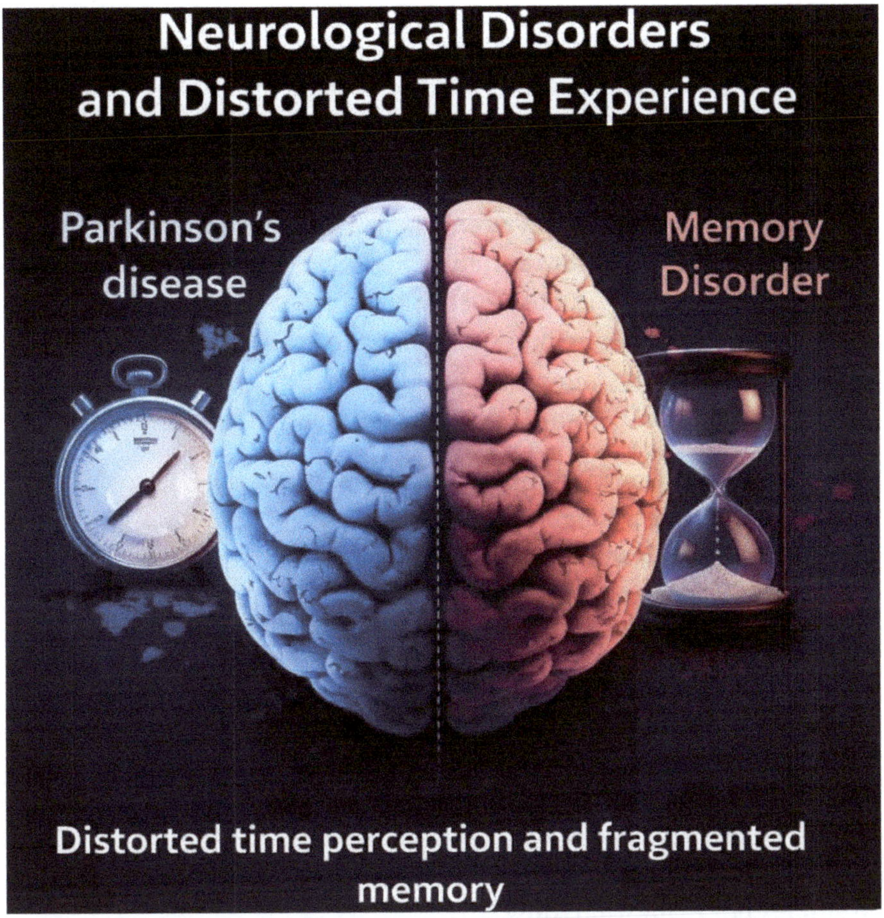

Neurological disorders offer powerful insights into how deeply time perception and memory are rooted in brain function. When neural systems responsible for timing, sequencing, and memory integration are disrupted, the subjective experience of time can change dramatically. These alterations reveal that psychological time is not an abstract concept but a direct outcome of neural integrity and coordination.

In movement-related neurological conditions, disruptions in internal timing mechanisms are common. Individuals may find it difficult to estimate durations, anticipate future events, or maintain a steady sense of rhythm. Everyday activities such as waiting, planning, or coordinating actions can feel unpredictable or disjointed. This occurs because neural circuits that normally regulate temporal intervals and sequencing lose their efficiency, leading to distorted judgments of how fast or slow time is passing.

Memory-related disorders produce a different, yet equally profound, distortion of temporal experience. When the ability to form or retrieve memories is impaired, the continuity between past, present, and future begins to fragment. Without reliable access to past experiences or the capacity to imagine future outcomes, individuals may feel psychologically anchored in the present moment. Time no longer unfolds as a coherent narrative but instead becomes a series of disconnected experiences.

These conditions demonstrate that a stable sense of time depends on the brain's ability to integrate memory, prediction, and attention. When this integration breaks down, temporal awareness loses its structure and depth. The resulting experience may feel either compressed, fragmented, or suspended, depending on which neural systems are affected.

Overall, distorted time perception in neurological disorders highlights the brain's central role in shaping how time is lived and understood. Such cases underscore that temporal experience is not merely measured by clocks but constructed by neural processes that give meaning to past memories and future possibilities.

Multiple Choice Questions (MCQs)

1. Which statement best describes how time perception is represented in the brain?

A. It is controlled by a single specialized "time centre"
B. It relies only on sensory input from the environment
C. It emerges from distributed neural networks across multiple

brain regions
D. It is independent of memory and attention

Correct Answer: C

2. Why do children often have difficulty accurately estimating time durations?

A. They lack emotional awareness
B. Their neural timing systems are fully developed
C. Their brain circuits for temporal integration are still maturing
D. They rely more on external clocks than internal timing

Correct Answer: C

3. What is the primary characteristic of memory functioning in adulthood compared to childhood?

A. Faster formation of new episodic memories
B. Greater emphasis on efficiency and selective encoding
C. Reduced reliance on long-term memory
D. Complete stability of all memory systems

Correct Answer: B

4. The "reminiscence bump" refers to the tendency of older adults to:

A. Forget childhood memories more rapidly
B. Recall recent events more vividly than past ones
C. Show enhanced memory only for emotionally negative events
D. Recall memories from adolescence and early adulthood more clearly

Correct Answer: D

5. What do studies on neuroplasticity in older adults demonstrate about time perception and memory?

A. Neural adaptation is impossible after middle age
B. Cognitive training has no measurable effect on temporal

awareness
C. Late-life learning can improve attention, memory, and subjective time experience
D. Time perception becomes entirely fixed in later life

Correct Answer: C

Short Answer Questions

1. What is meant by the term *distributed neural networks* in relation to time perception?
2. How does the role of the prefrontal cortex contribute to future-oriented thinking?
3. Why does memory encoding differ between childhood and adulthood?
4. Define the *reminiscence bump* and explain its significance in aging.
5. How does neuroplasticity influence temporal awareness across the lifespan?
6. In what way can memory disorders disrupt an individual's sense of past and future?

Long Answer Questions

1. Explain how time perception emerges from the interaction of multiple brain systems rather than a single neural centre.
2. Discuss the developmental changes in memory circuits from childhood through old age and their impact on temporal experience.
3. Analyse the role of neuroplasticity in maintaining and improving time perception during adulthood and later life.
4. Describe how neurological disorders can distort subjective time experience, using examples from movement or memory-related conditions.

5. Examine why memories from adolescence and early adulthood are often recalled more vividly in old age.
6. Evaluate the relationship between memory, attention, and temporal continuity in shaping psychological time across the lifespan.

8

Cultural, Social, and Evolutionary Perspectives on Psychological Time

8.1 Cultural Models of Time

Cultures differ significantly in how time is understood and valued. Some societies emphasize linear progression and punctuality, while others prioritize cyclical or event-based time. These cultural frameworks influence memory organization and life planning.

Human experience of time is not universal; it is shaped deeply by cultural beliefs, social practices, and collective values. Different cultures develop distinct "models of time" that guide how people organize daily life, remember the past, and plan for the future. These models influence not only behaviour but also psychological experiences such as stress, patience, urgency, and emotional connection.

In many industrialized societies, time is commonly viewed as **linear and sequential**. It is treated as a limited resource that moves forward in a straight line-from past to present to future. This perspective emphasizes punctuality, schedules, deadlines, and long-term planning. Individuals raised in such environments often learn to divide time into measurable units, leading to a strong focus on efficiency and productivity. As a result, people may feel constant pressure to "use time well," and delays can be experienced as anxiety-provoking or wasteful.

In contrast, other cultures understand time in a more **cyclical or event-based** manner. Instead of being governed by clocks, activities unfold according to natural rhythms, social interactions, or the completion of meaningful events. Time is experienced as repeating patterns rather than a one-way path. In these contexts, relationships, community obligations, and situational flexibility often take priority over strict schedules. Individuals from such cultures may experience time as more fluid, less stressful, and closely tied to social harmony rather than individual achievement.

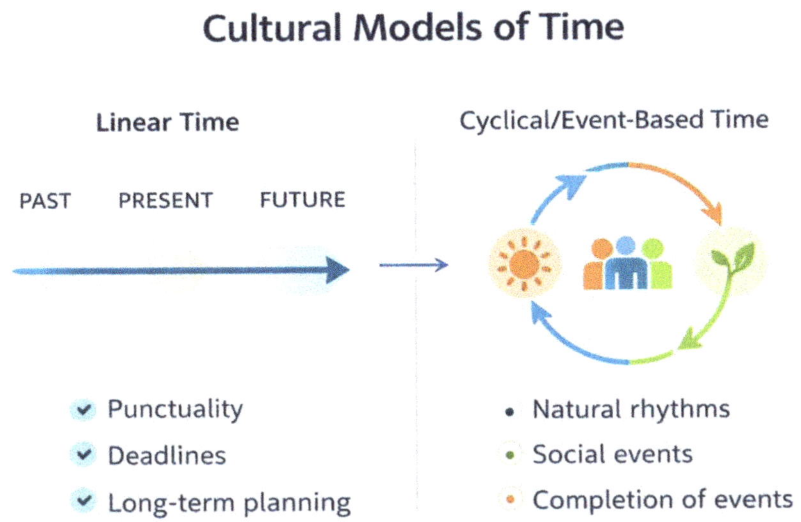

These cultural models also shape **memory organization and life planning** . Linear time cultures encourage people to structure memories chronologically and set clear future goals, while cyclical or relational cultures may recall experiences based on social significance or recurring traditions. Consequently, perceptions of time pressure, patience, and urgency vary widely across societies.

Overall, cultural models of time influence how individuals feel about deadlines, waiting, aging, and progress. Understanding these differences helps explain why time can feel rigid and demanding in some settings, yet relaxed and relational in others.

8.2 Social Roles and Temporal Identity

Social roles such as student, parent, or elder shape how individuals relate to time. Each role carries expectations tied to age and life stage.

An individual's relationship with time is intricately connected to the social roles they occupy throughout life. Roles such as student, employee, parent, caregiver, or elder are not only social identities but also temporal frameworks that organize daily routines, future expectations, and memories of the past. Each role carries implicit assumptions about how time should be used, valued, and prioritized.

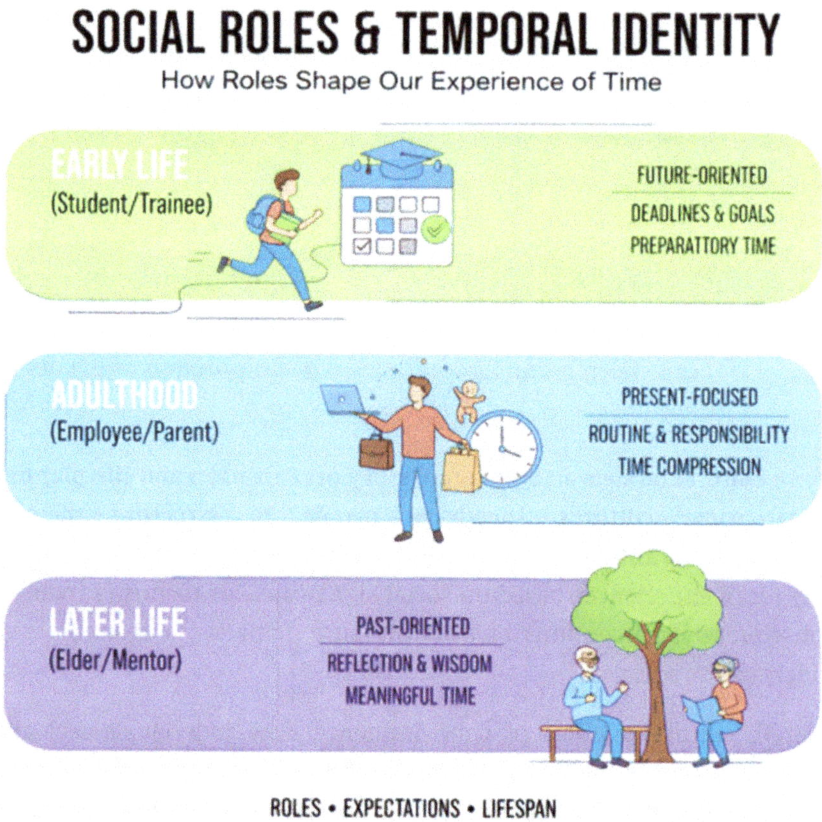

During early life stages, roles like **student or trainee** emphasize future-oriented thinking. Time is often structured around deadlines, examinations, and long-term goals. Individuals in these roles tend to view time as preparatory, with the present serving as a stepping stone toward anticipated achievements. This orientation strengthens planning skills but can also create pressure and a sense that meaningful life lies ahead rather than in the present.

In adulthood, roles such as **parent or professional** introduce dense temporal demands. Daily time becomes fragmented across responsibilities, schedules, and obligations. People in these roles often experience time as scarce and fast-moving, as attention is divided between work, family, and social expectations. Memories formed during this period are frequently linked to responsibilities rather than personal reflection, shaping how this life phase is later remembered.

A clear illustration of the link between social roles and temporal identity appears during **retirement transitions** . When the structured role of employment ends, individuals often face a sudden reorganization of time. For some, the loss of routine and externally imposed schedules creates disorientation, boredom, or a feeling of temporal emptiness. The absence of clear time markers can challenge one's sense of purpose and continuity.

For others, retirement brings **psychological liberation** . Freed from rigid schedules, individuals may experience time as expansive and self-directed. They can reframe their temporal identity around personal interests, relationships, and reflective activities. This shift demonstrates that time experience is not fixed but shaped by the meanings attached to social roles.

Overall, social context acts as a powerful mediator of temporal experience. As roles change, so does the way time is perceived, structured, and remembered, reinforcing the idea that temporal identity evolves across the lifespan rather than remaining constant.

8.3 Evolutionary Origins of Temporal Cognition

From an evolutionary standpoint, the ability to remember past events and anticipate future outcomes provided a survival advantage. Early humans relied on memory to locate resources and avoid danger, while future thinking enabled planning and cooperation.

The human capacity to think about time did not emerge by chance; it developed as an adaptive response to environmental challenges faced by early ancestors. From an evolutionary perspective, temporal cognition-the ability to recall the past and anticipate the future-offered significant survival benefits. Individuals who could learn from previous experiences and use that knowledge to guide future actions were better equipped to secure food, avoid threats, and adapt to changing conditions.

Memory played a central role in early human survival. Remembering the locations of water sources, seasonal food availability, and dangerous territories allowed groups to navigate their environment more effectively. Experiences of past success or failure shaped future behaviour, reducing repeated risks. Over time, this reliance on memory strengthened neural systems capable of storing, retrieving, and integrating experiences across extended periods.

Equally important was the evolution of **future-oriented thinking**. Anticipating outcomes enabled early humans to plan hunts, prepare tools, store food, and coordinate group activities. This capacity supported cooperation, as individuals could align their actions toward shared future goals. Planning ahead also allowed humans to delay immediate gratification in favour of long-term benefits, a trait that became essential for social living and cultural development.

This evolutionary background helps explain why humans possess an advanced form of **psychological time**. Unlike instinct-driven animals that respond primarily to immediate stimuli, humans can mentally revisit the past and imagine multiple possible futures. This reflective ability allows for storytelling, moral reasoning, goal setting, and complex decision-making.

In essence, temporal cognition reflects an evolutionary bridge between survival instincts and higher mental functions. The human mind's ability to integrate memory and foresight distinguishes psychological time as a uniquely advanced feature, shaping not only behaviour but also identity, culture, and long-term social organization.

Evolutionary Aspect	Role in Early Human Survival	Cognitive Function Developed	Psychological Significance
Memory of past events	Remembering locations of food, water, and danger	Episodic and associative memory	Enables learning from experience and avoiding repeated risks
Anticipation of future outcomes	Planning hunts, migrations, and shelter	Prospective thinking and foresight	Supports goal-setting and delayed gratification
Environmental adaptation	Adjusting behaviour to seasonal and climatic changes	Temporal pattern recognition	Helps predict recurring events and cycles
Social cooperation	Coordinating group actions and shared tasks	Collective planning and communication	Strengthens social bonds and group survival
Decision-making over time	Choosing long-term benefits over immediate rewards	Temporal evaluation and self-control	Forms the basis of reflective and purposeful behaviour

8.4 Intergenerational Transmission of Time Awareness

Temporal understanding is passed across generations through storytelling, rituals, and shared memory. Elders often serve as carriers of collective memory, linking personal time with historical continuity.

Human understanding of time is not formed solely through individual experience; it is also shaped and sustained through intergenerational exchange. Societies transmit temporal awareness from one generation to the next using cultural practices such as storytelling, rituals, ceremonies, and shared remembrance. Through these mechanisms, personal experiences become embedded within a broader historical and social timeline.

Elders play a central role in this process. As custodians of collective memory, they connect present generations to past events, traditions, and values. Their narratives often blend personal experiences with communal history, allowing younger members to situate their own lives within a longer temporal continuum. This linkage helps individuals perceive time not merely as a sequence of personal moments, but as an ongoing story that extends beyond their lifespan.

Storytelling is one of the most powerful tools for transmitting temporal knowledge. Through myths, legends, and historical accounts, societies preserve lessons from the past and project expectations for the future. These narratives organize time around meaning rather than strict chronology, emphasizing moral continuity, cultural identity, and shared purpose. Rituals further reinforce this awareness by marking recurring events-such as seasons, life transitions, or ancestral commemorations-thereby blending cyclical and linear conceptions of time.

Case studies from indigenous communities illustrate this process clearly. In many such societies, oral traditions maintain detailed knowledge of ancestry, land use, and historical change over centuries. Time is experienced as collective and enduring, rather than individual and fleeting. This long-term temporal perspective strengthens cultural resilience, helping communities maintain identity despite social or environmental disruptions.

Overall, intergenerational transmission highlights the **social dimension of psychological time** . Time awareness is not confined to the individual mind; it is cultivated through shared memory and cultural continuity. By linking past, present, and future across generations, societies ensure that temporal understanding remains a living, collective experience rather than a purely personal one.

Multiple Choice Questions (MCQs)

1. Which statement best describes cultural models of time?

a) Time perception is identical across all societies
b) Cultures differ in how time is structured, valued, and experienced
c) Time is determined only by biological rhythms
d) Cultural beliefs have no effect on time awareness
Answer: b

2. How do social roles influence an individual's experience of time?

a) Social roles eliminate subjective time perception
b) Social roles impose expectations that structure daily routines

and future orientation
c) Social roles affect only childhood time perception
d) Social roles have no relationship with memory or planning
Answer: b

3. Why did temporal cognition provide an evolutionary advantage to early humans?

a) It reduced emotional responses
b) It allowed humans to ignore immediate environmental threats
c) It supported learning from the past and planning for future survival needs
d) It eliminated instinctual behaviour entirely
Answer: c

4. What commonly occurs during retirement in relation to psychological time?

a) Time perception becomes completely objective
b) Daily time structure often changes, leading to either disorientation or freedom
c) Memory capacity immediately declines
d) Individuals lose awareness of future planning
Answer: b

5. How is time awareness transmitted across generations?

a) Through biological inheritance alone
b) Through formal education only
c) Through storytelling, rituals, and shared collective memory
d) Through individual introspection
Answer: c

Short Answer Questions

1. What is meant by a *cultural model of time*?

2. How do social roles influence daily time organization?

3. Why is retirement considered a critical transition in temporal identity?
4. How did memory contribute to survival in early human societies?
5. What role do elders play in the transmission of time awareness?
6. How does psychological time differ from instinct-driven behaviour?

Long Answer Questions

1. Discuss how different cultures conceptualize time and explain how these differences affect stress, planning, and memory organization.
2. Examine the relationship between social roles and temporal identity across the human lifespan, with suitable examples.
3. Explain the evolutionary origins of temporal cognition and its significance in distinguishing humans from other species.
4. Analyse retirement as a social transition and its impact on psychological time perception and self-identity.
5. Describe the process of intergenerational transmission of time awareness and its importance for cultural continuity and resilience.
6. Evaluate how cultural, social, and evolutionary factors together shape human psychological time, illustrating your answer with relevant examples.

9

The Future Mind – Technology, Longevity, and Temporal Consciousness

9.1 Digital Memory and the Externalization of Time

Modern technology has transformed how memories are stored and revisited. Digital photographs, social media timelines, and cloud storage externalize memory, altering how individuals relate to their past.

In contemporary life, digital technology has fundamentally reshaped how human beings record, recall, and interpret time. Memories that were once stored primarily in the mind are now increasingly preserved outside the self through digital artifacts such as photographs, videos, emails, social media posts, and cloud-based archives. This process, often described as the externalization of memory, changes the relationship individuals have with their past by making personal history continuously accessible, searchable, and revisit able.

Digital memory alters temporal experience by transforming remembrance from an internal, reconstructive act into a retrieval-based activity. Instead of relying on mental recall, individuals can scroll through timelines, search archives, or revisit notifications to reconnect with earlier moments. As a result, the past becomes less distant and more immediate, sometimes collapsing the psychological boundary between “then” and “now.” Events that might once have faded or been reshaped by emotion and reflection remain frozen in digital form, influencing how people interpret their life narratives.

However, this convenience also shifts cognitive habits. Research in cognitive psychology suggests that when information is reliably stored externally, people tend to remember *where* the information is located rather than the information itself. This phenomenon changes temporal cognition by reducing the need for deep encoding and long-term internal memory formation. Time, in this sense, becomes organized around access points-folders, dates, notifications, and platforms-rather than lived continuity.

Moreover, digital memory can fragment the experience of time. Constant reminders, "memories" features, and algorithm-driven resurfacing of past events can interrupt present awareness, pulling individuals backward into earlier moments without intentional reflection. While this can strengthen identity by reinforcing continuity, it can also create emotional dissonance when past experiences reappear unexpectedly.

Overall, digital memory extends human capacity to preserve time but reshapes how time is psychologically experienced. Rather than flowing primarily through personal recollection, time increasingly exists as an external archive-structured, searchable, and persistent-fundamentally altering how individuals understand their past, navigate the present, and anticipate the future.

9.2 Artificial Intelligence and Temporal Decision-Making

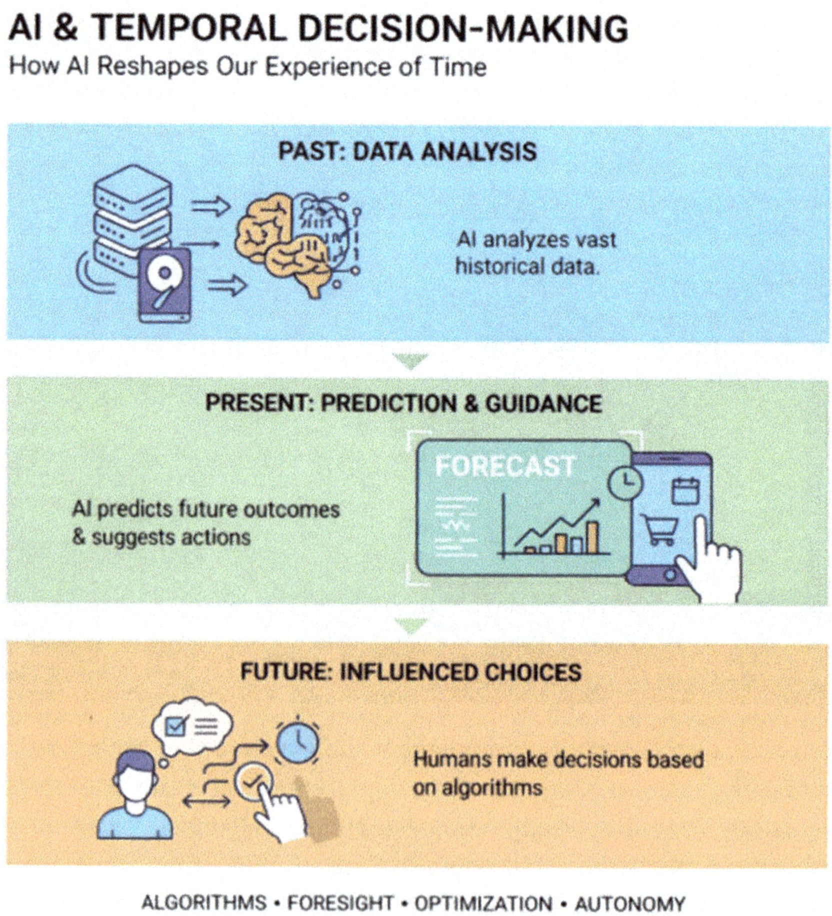

AI systems increasingly assist with planning, prediction, and decision-making, influencing human time orientation.

Artificial intelligence has become a powerful mediator of how humans think about time, particularly in planning, forecasting, and everyday decision-making. By analysing vast amounts of past data, AI systems generate predictions that guide future-oriented choices, subtly reshaping human temporal orientation. Instead of relying solely on personal judgment or intuition, individuals increasingly depend on algorithmic suggestions that anticipate outcomes before actions are taken.

AI-driven recommendation systems are a clear illustration of this shift. Platforms that suggest what to watch, read, buy, or listen to base their guidance on patterns from prior behaviour. As a result, the future is not approached as an open field of possibilities but as a statistically inferred continuation of the past. This can make decision-making faster and more efficient, yet it also narrows the temporal horizon by favouring familiarity over exploration. Over time, individuals may come to trust predictive systems more than their own forward-looking imagination.

Navigation technologies provide a practical and widely experienced example of AI's influence on temporal decision-making. Predictive routing algorithms calculate the fastest or most efficient path by forecasting traffic, delays, and environmental conditions. This reduces uncertainty and saves time, reinforcing a purposeful perception of the future. However, such optimization can limit spontaneous detours, exploratory travel, or unplanned experiences. Time becomes something to be minimized and controlled rather than discovered or experienced organically.

This growing reliance on AI raises important questions about human autonomy and temporal agency. When intelligent systems anticipate needs and pre-structure future actions, individuals may become passive recipients of algorithmic foresight. Decision-making shifts from active temporal reasoning-imagining, weighing, and choosing futures-to accepting recommended trajectories. While this can enhance productivity and reduce cognitive load, it may weaken the human capacity for long-term reflection, creative planning, and adaptive thinking.

In essence, artificial intelligence transforms time from a subjective, flexible dimension into a managed and optimized resource. As AI systems continue to evolve, the challenge lies in balancing efficiency with autonomy-ensuring that technological assistance enhances human temporal awareness without replacing the deeply human ability to imagine, shape, and redefine the future.

9.3 Longevity, Aging, and Extended Psychological Time

Advances in healthcare are extending human lifespan, altering how individuals perceive their future. Longer lives encourage extended planning horizons but may also intensify existential concerns about meaning and purpose.

Advances in healthcare, nutrition, and preventive medicine have significantly increased human life expectancy, reshaping how individuals relate to time across the lifespan. As people anticipate longer lives, their perception of the future expands beyond traditional milestones such as retirement or late adulthood. Psychological time-the subjective sense of how much life remains-stretches forward, encouraging longer planning horizons and a reorganization of life goals.

Extended longevity changes the meaning of aging itself. Rather than viewing later life as a period of decline, many individuals now see it as a stage for reinvention, learning, and continued contribution. This shift alters future orientation: people are more likely to invest in education, skill development, and long-term projects well into midlife and beyond. Time is no longer compressed toward an endpoint but redistributed into multiple phases of growth, rest, and renewal.

However, an extended future can also intensify existential reflection. When life is longer, questions about purpose, fulfilment, and identity gain greater psychological weight. Individuals may experience pressure to "use time well," leading to concerns about wasted years or unfulfilled potential. The awareness of having more time does not always bring comfort; instead, it can amplify the challenge of defining meaning across decades rather than years.

Case examples of individuals pursuing second or even third careers later in life illustrate this transformation vividly. Professionals who retrain in their 50s or 60s-such as engineers becoming educators or corporate leaders moving into social work-demonstrate how extended longevity reshapes identity. Their sense of self is no longer anchored to a single lifelong role but evolves dynamically, guided by an expanded sense of future possibility. In these cases, psychological time supports reinvention rather than closure.

Overall, increased lifespan expands psychological time and demands new frameworks for life planning. Traditional linear models of education, work, and retirement become less relevant, replaced by cyclical or modular life structures. As longevity continues to grow, individuals and societies must rethink how meaning, productivity, and fulfilment are distributed across extended human time, ensuring that longer lives are not only lived longer, but lived well.

9.4 Ethical and Psychological Implications of Temporal Enhancement

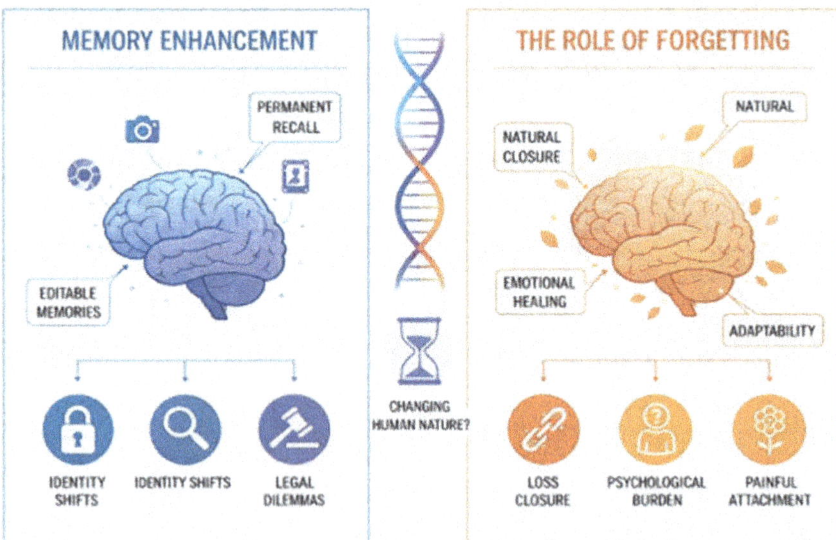

Technologies that enhance memory or slow cognitive aging raise ethical and psychological questions. If memories can be edited or preserved indefinitely, the nature of forgetting-and thus psychological closure-may change.

Technologies designed to enhance memory, preserve cognition, or slow psychological aging introduce profound ethical and psychological challenges. As human beings gain the ability to record, modify, or indefinitely store memories, the traditional relationship between time, forgetting, and emotional healing begins to shift. Forgetting has long played a vital role in psychological well-being by allowing individuals to distance themselves from painful experiences and achieve a sense of closure. When memories become permanent or editable, this natural process may be disrupted.

From a psychological perspective, the inability to forget could intensify emotional burdens. Traumatic or regretful experiences, when continuously accessible or vividly preserved, may prevent emotional resolution and prolong distress. Conversely, the selective editing of memories raises concerns about authenticity and identity. Personal identity is shaped not only by what is remembered, but also by what fades over time. Altering this balance risks creating fragmented or artificially curated selves that lack emotional continuity.

Ethically, temporal enhancement technologies raise questions of fairness, consent, and responsibility. Access to memory enhancement or cognitive preservation may be uneven, deepening social inequalities between those who can afford such interventions and those who cannot. There are also concerns about autonomy: individuals may feel pressured to enhance their memory or cognitive lifespan to remain competitive, even if such interventions conflict with their psychological comfort or values.

The concept of psychological closure is especially at risk in an era of temporal enhancement. Closure depends on the mind's ability to reinterpret, soften, or release past experiences. If technology continuously revives or preserves moments in their original intensity, individuals may struggle to move forward emotionally. Time may cease to feel progressive and instead become repetitive, trapping people in cycles of revisitation rather than growth.

Looking ahead, the evolution of human psychology will depend on how societies integrate temporal enhancement technologies with ethical restraint and emotional wisdom. Technological control over time-related processes must be balanced with respect for mental health, narrative coherence, and the human need for meaning. Preserving emotional depth, personal growth, and the capacity to let go will be essential if technological advances are to support-not undermine-the psychological integrity of future generations.

Multiple Choice Questions (MCQs)

1. How does digital memory primarily alter human temporal experience?

A. By weakening emotional connections to the past
B. By replacing biological memory entirely
C. By externalizing personal history into accessible archives
D. By eliminating the need for future planning

Correct Answer: C

2. What cognitive shift commonly occurs when individuals rely heavily on digital storage for information?

A. Enhanced long-term emotional recall
B. Improved imaginative future thinking
C. Remembering information more deeply
D. Remembering where information is stored rather than the content

Correct Answer: D

3. In what way do AI-driven recommendation systems influence temporal decision-making?

A. They expand future possibilities equally
B. They predict random outcomes

C. They discourage planning
D. They shape future choices based on past behaviour

Correct Answer: D

4. How does increased human longevity most significantly affect psychological time?

A. It shortens future planning horizons
B. It eliminates concerns about aging
C. It expands future-oriented identity and life planning
D. It reduces the need for personal growth

Correct Answer: C

5. Why is the ability to forget considered psychologically important in the context of temporal enhancement technologies?

A. It prevents memory accuracy
B. It supports emotional closure and mental well-being
C. It weakens personal identity
D. It slows cognitive development

Correct Answer: B

Short Answer Questions

1. What is meant by the *externalization of memory* in the digital age?
2. How do recommendation algorithms influence human future-oriented thinking?
3. In what way does navigation technology reduce uncertainty in temporal decision-making?
4. How does increased life expectancy expand psychological time?
5. Why is forgetting considered essential for emotional closure?
6. What is temporal agency, and how can technology affect it?

Long Answer Questions

1. Discuss how digital technologies have transformed human memory and altered the subjective experience of time.
2. Examine the role of artificial intelligence in shaping planning, prediction, and temporal decision-making in everyday life.
3. Analyse how extended longevity influence's identity formation and future orientation across adulthood.
4. Explain the ethical implications of memory enhancement and cognitive preservation technologies on personal identity.
5. Evaluate the psychological consequences of reduced forgetting in an era of permanent digital memory.
6. Critically discuss how societies can balance technological temporal enhancement with human emotional depth and narrative coherence.

References

Chapter 1: Time as a Psychological Construct

1. Block, R. A., Hancock, P. A., & Zakay, D. (2010). How cognitive load affects duration judgments: A meta-analytic review. *Psychological Bulletin*, 136(3), 430–451. https://doi.org/10.1037/a0019540

2. Zakay, D., & Block, R. A. (1997). Temporal cognition. *Current Directions in Psychological Science*, 6(1), 12–16. https://doi.org/10.1111/1467-8721.ep11512604

3. Eagleman, D. M. (2008). Human time perception and its illusions. *Current Opinion in Neurobiology*, 18(2), 131–136. https://doi.org/10.1016/j.conb.2008.06.002

Chapter 2: Memory and the Architecture of the Mind

1. Tulving, E. (2002). Episodic memory: From mind to brain. *Annual Review of Psychology*, 53, 1–25. https://doi.org/10.1146/annurev.psych.53.100901.135114

2. Baddeley, A. (2003). Working memory: Looking back and looking forward. *Nature Reviews Neuroscience*, 4(10), 829–839. https://doi.org/10.1038/nrn1201

3. Suddendorf, T., & Corballis, M. C. (2007). The evolution of foresight: What is mental time travel? *Behavioural and Brain Sciences*, 30(3), 299–351. https://doi.org/10.1017/S0140525X07001975

Chapter 3: Childhood and the Formation of Temporal Awareness

1. Friedman, W. J. (2003). The development of a differentiated sense of the past and future. *Advances in Child Development and Behaviour*, 31, 229–269. https://doi.org/10.1016/S0065-2407(03)31005-1

2. Nelson, K., & Fivush, R. (2004). The emergence of autobiographical memory: A social cultural developmental theory. *Psychological Review*, 111(2), 486–511. https://doi.org/10.1037/0033-295X.111.2.486

3. McCormack, T., & Hoerl, C. (2008). Temporal concepts and the development of episodic memory. *Psychological Bulletin*, 134(1), 133–153. https://doi.org/10.1037/0033-2909.134.1.133

Chapter 4: Adolescence, Identity, and Accelerated Time Perception

1. Blakemore, S. J., & Mills, K. L. (2014). Is adolescence a sensitive period for sociocultural processing? *Annual Review of Psychology*, 65, 187–207. https://doi.org/10.1146/annurev-psych-010213-115202
2. Erikson, E. H. (1968). *Identity: Youth and crisis*. New York: W. W. Norton & Company.
3. Steinberg, L. (2008). A social neuroscience perspective on adolescent risk-taking. *Developmental Review*, 28(1), 78–106. https://doi.org/10.1016/j.dr.2007.08.002

Chapter 5: Adulthood, Routine, and the Compression of Time

1. James, W. (1890). *The principles of psychology*. New York: Henry Holt and Company.
2. Csikszentmihalyi, M. (1990). *Flow: The psychology of optimal experience*. New York: Harper & Row.
3. Wittmann, M., & Lehnhoff, S. (2005). Age effects in perception of time. *Psychological Reports*, 97(3), 921–935.

Chapter 6: Aging, Memory Transformation, and Psychological Adaptation

1. Park, D. C., & Reuter-Lorenz, P. (2009). The adaptive brain: Aging and neurocognitive scaffolding. *Annual Review of Psychology*, 60, 173–196. https://doi.org/10.1146/annurev.psych.59.103006.093656
2. Rubin, D. C., Wetzler, S. E., & Nebes, R. D. (1986). Autobiographical memory across the lifespan. *Human Development*, 29(1), 1–12. https://doi.org/10.1159/000273042
3. Baltes, P. B., & Baltes, M. M. (1990). *Successful aging: Perspectives from the behavioural sciences*. Cambridge University Press.

Chapter 7: The Neuroscience of Time and Memory Across the Lifespan

1. Buhusi, C. V., & Meck, W. H. (2005). What makes us tick? *Nature Reviews Neuroscience*, 6(10), 755–765. https://doi.org/10.1038/nrn1764
2. Nyberg, L., et al. (2012). Memory aging and brain maintenance. *Trends in Cognitive Sciences*, 16(5), 292–305. https://doi.org/10.1016/j.tics.2012.04.005
3. Draganski, B., et al. (2004). Neuroplasticity: Changes in grey matter induced by training. *Nature*, 427, 311–312. https://doi.org/10.1038/427311a

Chapter 8: Cultural, Social, and Evolutionary Perspectives on Psychological Time

1. Hall, E. T. (1983). *The dance of life: The other dimension of time*. Anchor Press.
2. Levine, R. (1997). *A geography of time*. Basic Books.
3. Tomasello, M. (2014). *A natural history of human thinking*. Harvard University Press.

Chapter 9: The Future Mind – Technology, Longevity, and Temporal Consciousness

1. Sparrow, B., Liu, J., & Wegner, D. M. (2011). Google effects on memory. *Science*, 333(6043), 776–778.
2. Clark, A., & Chalmers, D. (1998). The extended mind. *Analysis*, 58(1), 7–19. https://doi.org/10.1093/analys/58.1.7
3. Harari, Y. N. (2017). *Homo Deus: A brief history of tomorrow*. Harper.

Appendix

1. Glossary of Key Terms

Psychological Time
The subjective experience of time as perceived by the human mind, influenced by cognition, emotion, memory, and context rather than objective measurement.

Temporal Perception
The cognitive ability to sense, estimate, and interpret the passage and duration of time.

Mental Time Travel
The capacity to mentally revisit past experiences or imagine future scenarios, relying on episodic memory and foresight.

Episodic Memory
A form of long-term memory that stores personal experiences along with their temporal and emotional context.

Semantic Memory
Long-term memory related to general knowledge, concepts, and facts that are not tied to specific time or place.

Reminiscence Bump
A phenomenon in which older adults recall a disproportionate number of memories from adolescence and early adulthood.

Neuroplasticity
The brain's ability to reorganize itself by forming new neural connections throughout life.

Temporal Compression
The subjective feeling that time passes more quickly, often associated with routine and reduced novelty.

Future Discounting
The tendency to undervalue future outcomes compared to immediate rewards.

Extended Mind
The idea that cognitive processes can extend beyond the brain to include external tools such as notebooks or digital devices.

2. Data Sources and Datasets

The following **authentic and reputable data sources** support research on time perception, memory, aging, and cognition:

1. **Human Connectome Project (HCP)**
   Large-scale neuroimaging datasets exploring brain structure and cognitive function.
   Source: National Institutes of Health (NIH)

2. **UK Biobank Cognitive Aging Dataset**
   Longitudinal data on memory, reaction time, and psychological aging.
   Source: UK Biobank

3. **National Institute on Aging (NIA) Cognitive Studies**
   Open datasets on aging, memory decline, and lifespan cognition.
   Source: U.S. National Institutes of Health

4. **Cambridge Centre for Ageing and Neuroscience (Cam-CAN)**
   Multimodal datasets on cognitive aging across adulthood.

5. **World Values Survey (WVS)**
   Cultural data useful for studying societal differences in time orientation and memory narratives.

3. Tools and Frameworks

Cognitive Psychology Frameworks

- Information Processing Model

- Lifespan Development Theory
- Socioemotional Selectivity Theory
- Constructivist Memory Models

Neuroscientific Tools

- Functional Magnetic Resonance Imaging (fMRI)
- Electroencephalography (EEG)
- Diffusion Tensor Imaging (DTI)

Psychological Assessment Instruments

- Time Estimation Tasks
- Autobiographical Memory Interview (AMI)
- Cognitive Reflection Tests
- Delay Discounting Tasks

Analytical and Research Tools

- SPSS and R for cognitive data analysis
- MATLAB for neural timing models
- Qualitative narrative analysis for life-story research

4. References for Further Reading

The following verified and authoritative works provide deeper insight into themes explored in the book:

- Block, R. A., & Zakay, D. (1997). Temporal cognition. *Current Directions in Psychological Science.*
- Tulving, E. (2002). Episodic memory: From mind to brain. *Annual Review of Psychology.*

- Suddendorf, T., & Corballis, M. (2007). Mental time travel. *Behavioural and Brain Sciences.*
- Carstensen, L. L. (2006). Time perspective and development. *Science.*
- Eagleman, D. M. (2008). Human time perception. *Current Opinion in Neurobiology.*
- Park, D. C., & Reuter-Lorenz, P. (2009). Cognitive aging. *Annual Review of Psychology.*
- Clark, A., & Chalmers, D. (1998). The extended mind. *Analysis.*

5. Future Directions in Psychological Time Research

Future research on psychological time is expected to move toward **integrative and technology-informed approaches** . Key directions include:

- **AI-assisted memory augmentation** and its ethical implications
- **Digital life-logging** and its impact on autobiographical memory
- **Longevity psychology** , addressing extended lifespans and temporal identity
- **Cross-cultural temporal cognition** , especially in non-Western societies
- **Neuroethical questions** surrounding memory enhancement and erasure
- **Temporal well-being**, focusing on slowing perceived time through mindfulness and novelty

These directions suggest that time perception will remain central to understanding future human psychological evolution.

6. Summary of Key Points

- Human experience of time is **psychological, flexible, and deeply subjective**.

- Memory functions as the **bridge between past, present, and future**.
- Time perception changes significantly across **childhood, adolescence, adulthood, and aging**.
- Emotional intensity and novelty shape how time is remembered.
- Cultural and social contexts influence temporal orientation.
- Neuroscience reveals that time perception emerges from **distributed brain systems**.
- Technology is redefining how humans store, recall, and imagine time.
- Psychological evolution depends not on time itself, but on **how the mind experiences it**.

ABOUT THE AUTHOR

Dr. Anu Kant Mital is an eminent psychiatrist, academic, and global mental health consultant with over three decades of experience in clinical psychiatry and psychological sciences. A graduate of Grant Medical College, Mumbai, he holds an M.D. in Psychiatry, a Ph.D. in Psychology from MAG H University (UK), and an M.A. in Psychology. His extensive training spans clinical hypnotherapy, family therapy (UK), criminology, and biomedical ethics. Dr. Mital has served as a UNESCO Unit Head in Biomedical Ethics (Haifa) and as an External Consultant with the United Nations CISMU. He is currently a Consultant Psychiatrist at several prestigious institutions including Jupiter Hospital, Masina Hospital, and Godbole Heart Hospital. He has held academic leadership roles such as Dean at FIAMC Biomedical Ethics Centre and in the past as the Professor of Psychiatry at R.G. Medical College. His international exposure includes service within the UK NHS and observation at the University of Berne, Switzerland.

10. E-LIBRAIRIE – France (French online bookstore)
11. Everand – India (Everand Book Distributor is based in India)
12. EXLIBRIS – Switzerland
13. Fable – United Kingdom (UK/Europe digital subscription book service)
14. Flipkart – India
15. GANDHI.com – Mexico (Librerías Gandhi)
16. Google Book – United States (Google LLC)
17. Google Audio Book – United States (Google LLC)
18. IBS.IT – Italy Wikipedia
19. Indigo – Canada
20. Kobo – Canada Wikipedia
21. Kindle – United States (Amazon product)
22. LAFELTRINELLI – Italy Wikipedia
23. Lehmanns – Germany
24. Lulu – United States
25. MORAWA – Austria
26. Rakuten Japan – Japan (Rakuten)
27. Smashwords – United States
28. Tolino / Thalia – Germany (Tolino is a German-language eBook ecosystem, Thalia DE)

29. Vivlio – France

30. Saxo – Denmark (Saxo.com)

31. YES24 – South Korea

and others.

🎁 You will receive 20 physical author copies FREE to your Indian address.

⭐ You can also receive 5 book reviews:

* 3 reviews by eminent university professors

* 2 reviews from your own group/colleagues/seniors/teachers

www.books.wissira.us

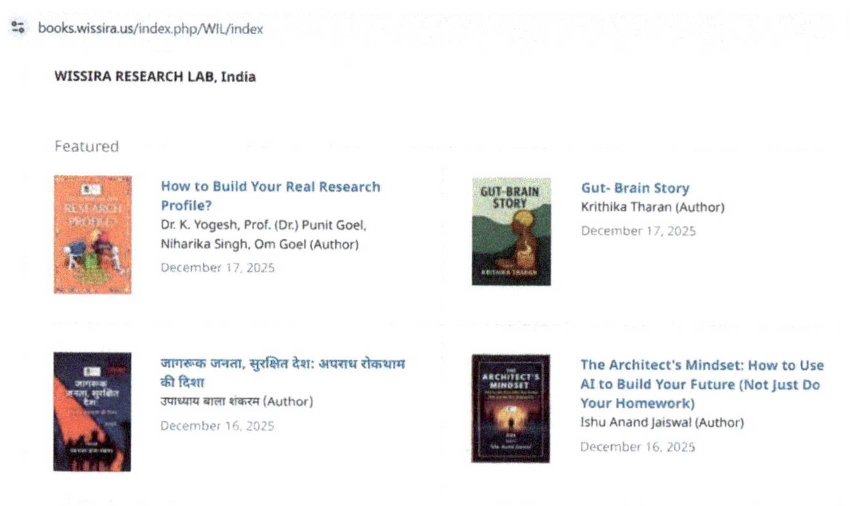

www.books.wissira.us

DOI: https://doi.org/10.63345/book.wrl.2512000324

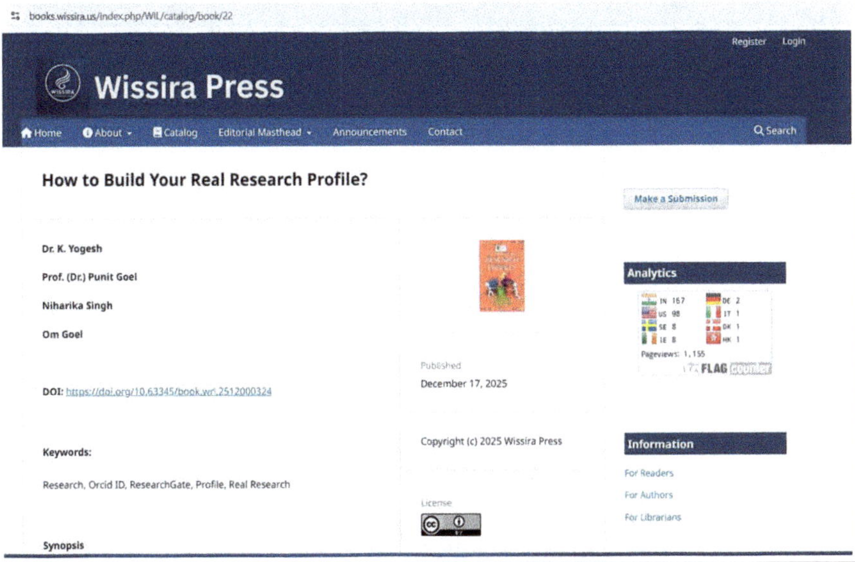

https://books.wissira.us/index.php/WIL/login

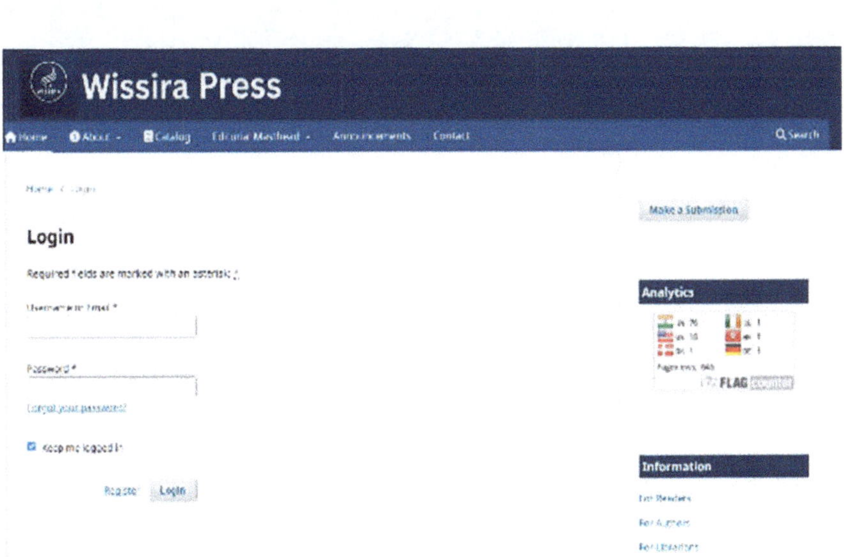

https://books.wissira.us/index.php/WIL/catalog
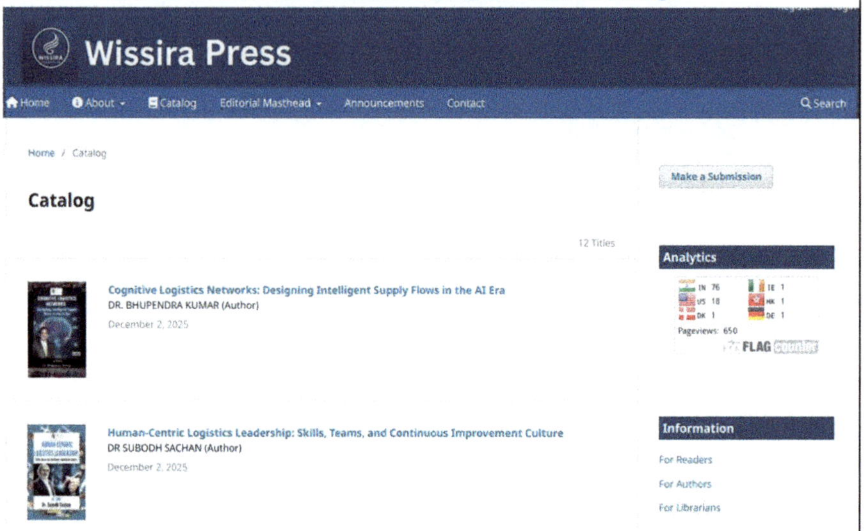
https://books.wissira.us/index.php/WIL/about/contact
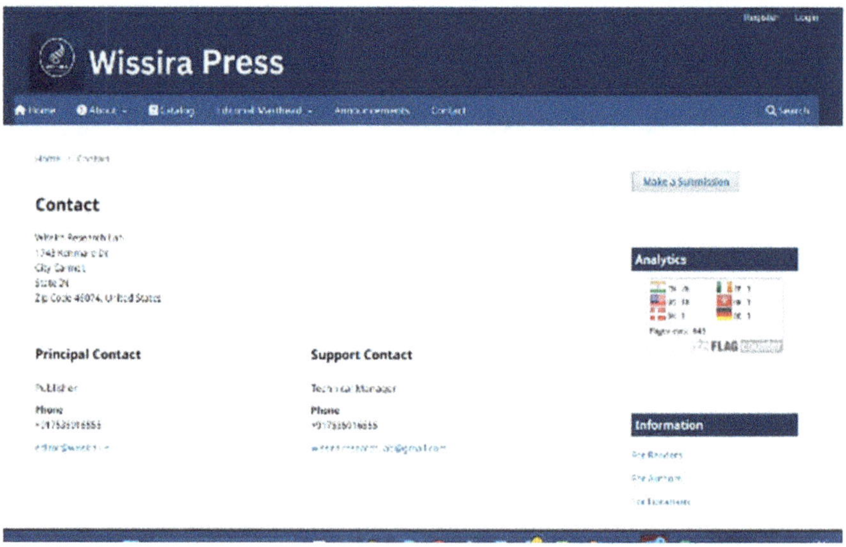
https://www.amazon.in/dp/B0G7MQFD2L

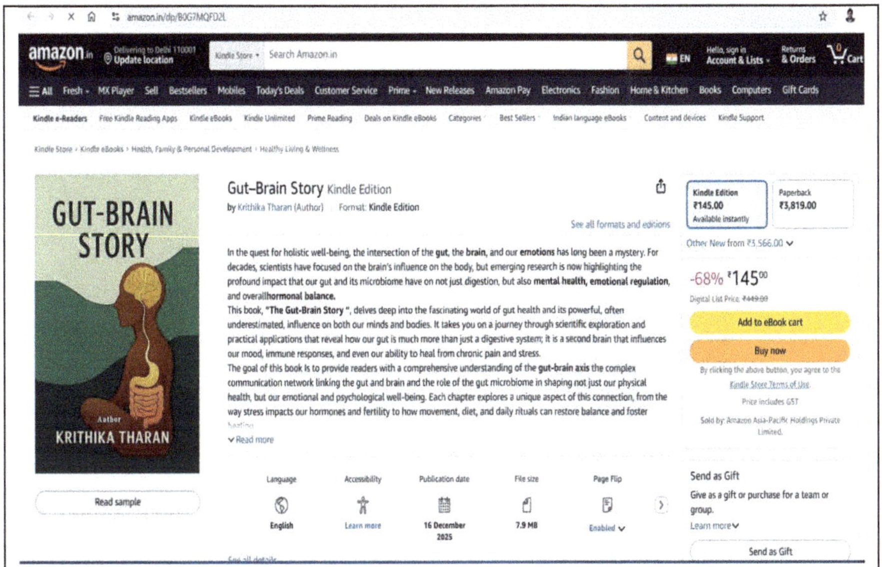

https://books.apple.com/us/book/the-architects-mindset-how-to-use-ai-to-build-your/id6756545876

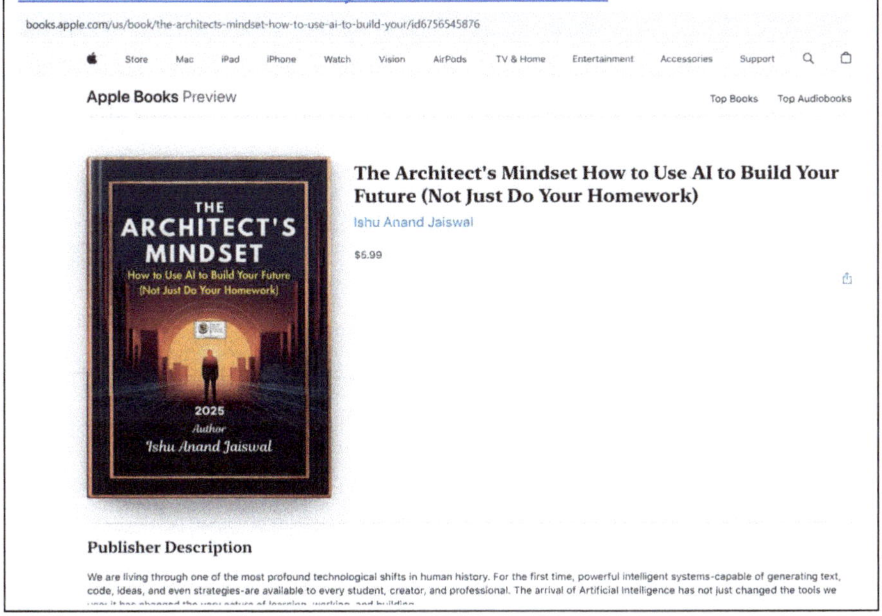

Flipkart:
https://tinyurl.com/WissieaPressBook250306Human

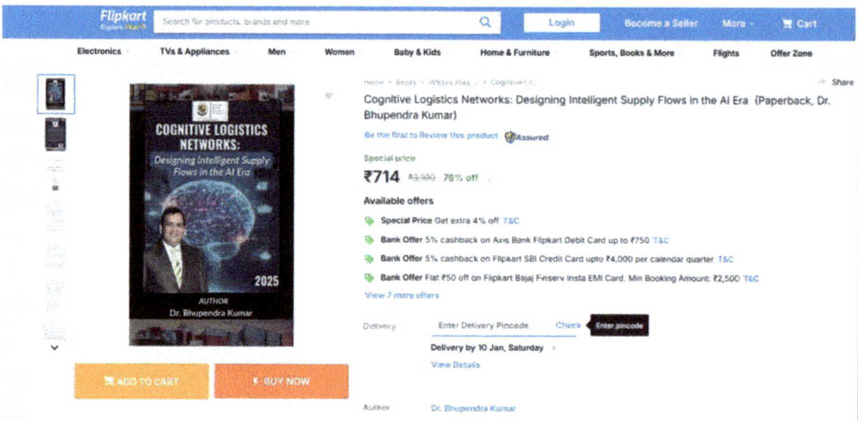

https://play.google.com/store/audiobooks/details?id=AQAAAEAa9DeoPM

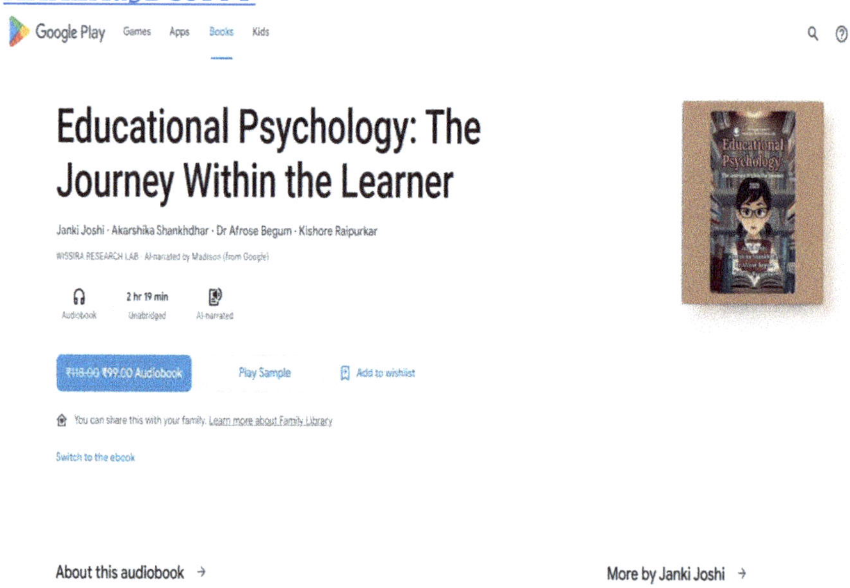

https://shop.vivlio.com/product/9798232547615_9798232547615_10020/human-centric-logistics-leadership-skills-teams-and-continuous-improvement-culture

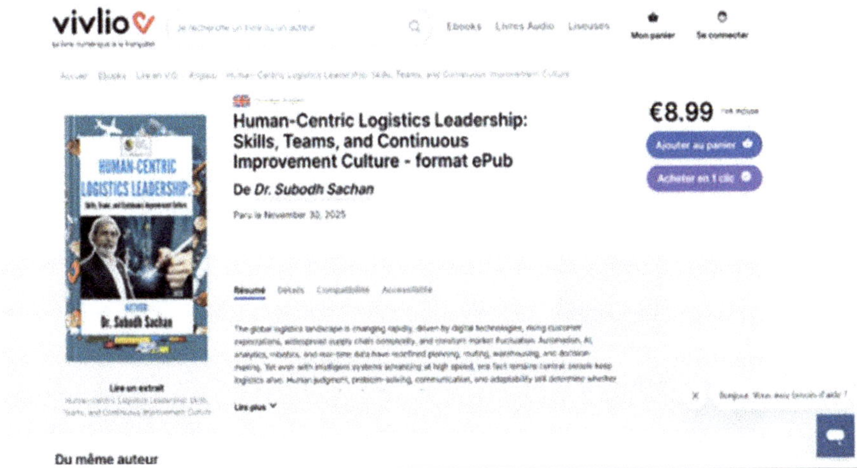

https://www.kobo.com/in/en/ebook/from-shakespeare-to-tagore-reinterpreting-english-literature-through-indian-sensibility?sId=070486d4-8aef-4220-a1d2-26bb2ba8ecb6&ssId=3FJLsnB4eTMdnS31kaTcM

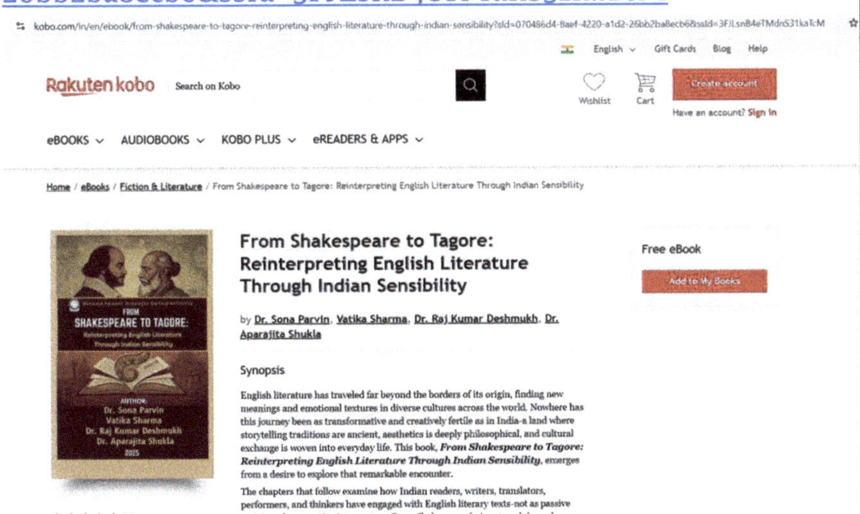

https://fable.co/book/x-9798230804772

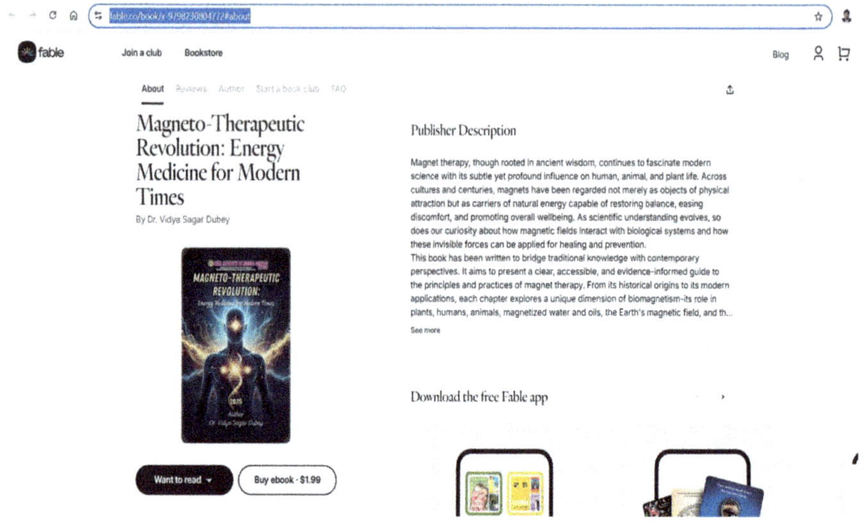

https://www.lulu.com/shop/dr-subodh-sachan/human-centric-logistics-leadership/ebook/product-rmj4erq.html?q=Human-Centric+Logistics+Leadership%3A+Skills%2C+Teams%2C+and+Continuous+Improvement+Culture&page=1&pageSize=

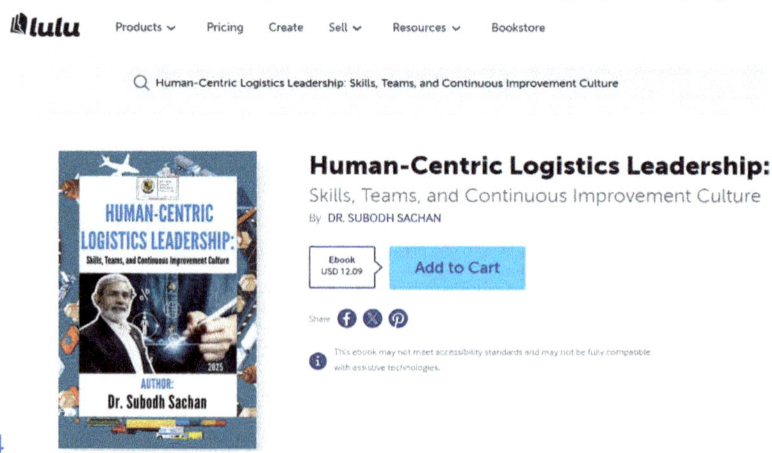

4

https://play.google.com/store/audiobooks/details?id=AQAAAEDqoRHh6M

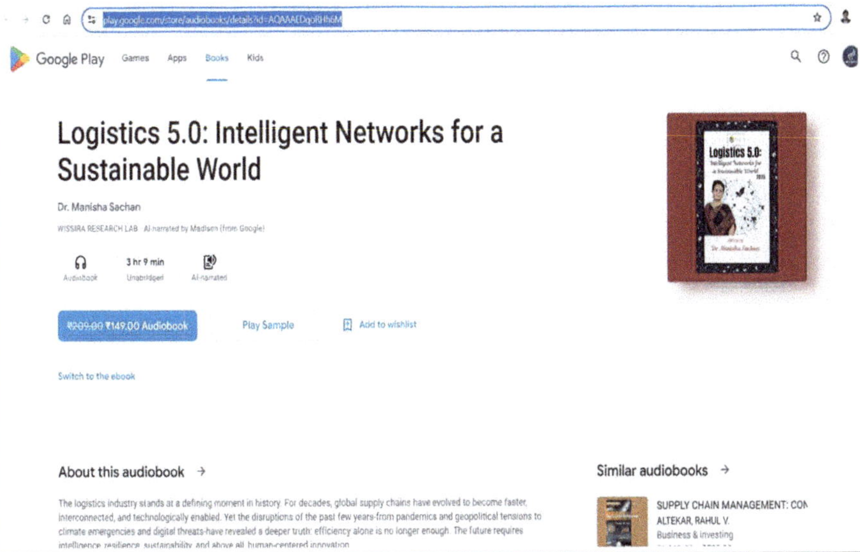

https://play.google.com/store/books/details?id=TbmfEQAAQBAJ

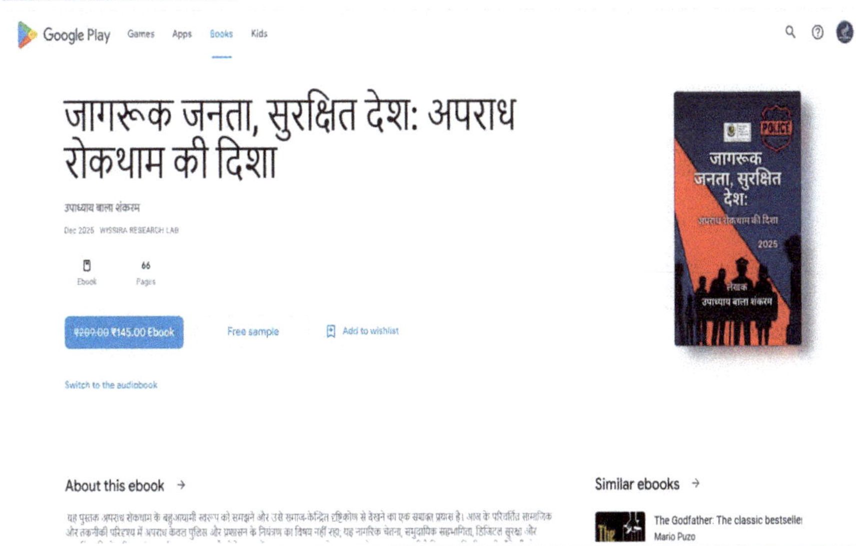

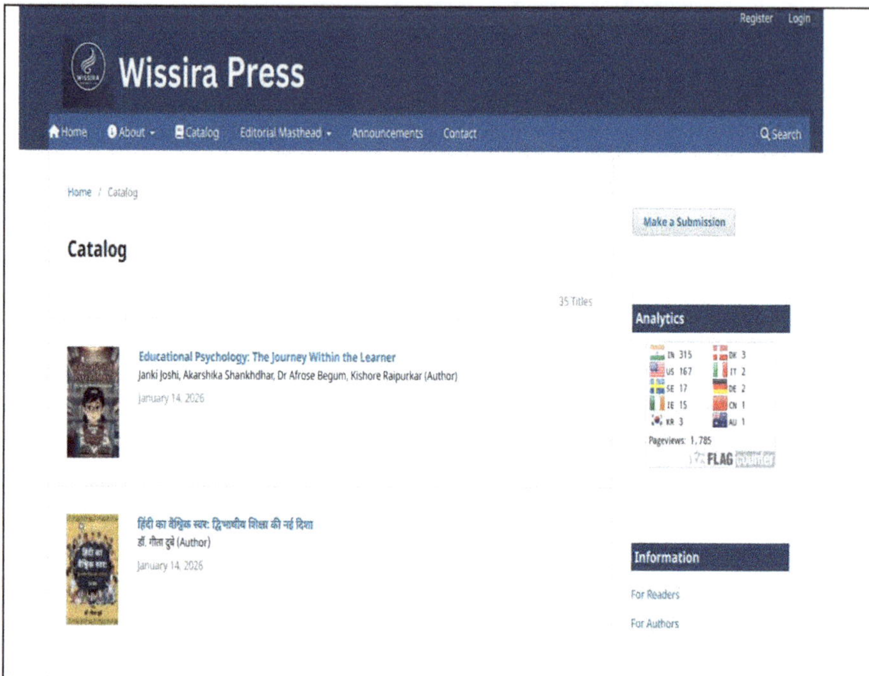

https://www.smashwords.com/books/view/1943936

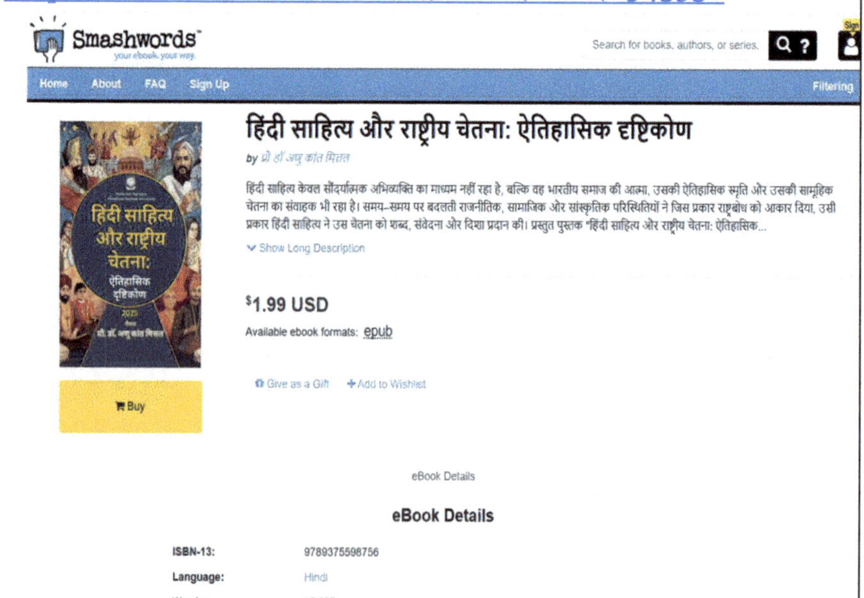

Analytics

IN	135	IT	1
US	84	DK	1
SE	8	HK	1
IE	8	DE	1

Pageviews: 1,012

FLAG counter

Amazon Kindle

Amazon

Flipkart

LULU

Apple Books

Barnes & Nobles

Everand

Fable

Kobo

Information

For Readers

For Authors

For Librarians

Keywords

sustain long-term operational excellence.

Across the nine chapters of this work, readers will find a structured and practical approach to understanding how leadership influences logistics outcomes. Beginning with the foundations of human-centric leadership, the book explores essential competencies such as communication, empathy, decision-making, and ethical responsibility-skills that enable leaders to build credibility and trust in high-pressure environments. It then moves deeper into the dynamics of teamwork, motivation, and empowerment, highlighting how resilient and collaborative teams become the backbone of

Smashwords

Tolino

Vivlio

Google Books
